STRIPPED BARE

STRIPPED BARE

*The 12 Truths
That Will Help You
Land the Very Best
Black Man*

LaDAWN BLACK

ONE WORLD

BALLANTINE • NEW YORK

To JB, for love and motivation
To Alec, for inspiration and possibility

A One World Books Trade Paperback Edition

Copyright © 2003, 2005 by LaDawn Black

Published in the United States by One World Books,
an imprint of The Random House Publishing Group,
a division of Random House, Inc., New York.
Originally published in different form by Xlibris
Morris Publishing, Philadelphia, in 2003.

ONE WORLD is a registered trademark and the One World colophon is a
trademark of Random House, Inc.

Library of Congress Cataloging-in-Publication Data

Black, LaDawn.

Stripped bare : the 12 truths that will help you land the very best black
man / by LaDawn Black.

p. cm.

ISBN 0-345-48366-9

1. Man-woman relationships—United States. 2. African American
women—Psychology. 3. African American women—Sexual behavior.
I. Title.

HQ801.B613 2006

306.73'089'96073—dc22   2005049801

Printed in the United States of America

www.oneworldbooks.net

2   4   6   8   9   7   5   3   1

Book design by Lisa Sloane

ACKNOWLEDGMENTS

The last two years have been the most exciting years of growth in my life. The success of *Stripped Bare* as a self-published project was the direct result of so many people stepping in and giving me great advice and professional assistance. I want to thank all of my friends and family who bought the book just because. Special thanks to F. Cobb for having one of the greatest reader networks ever and moving books for me like crazy. You gave me the confidence to believe that the book was really a great tool for women looking for great love.

I have been so lucky to have become involved with so many marvelous business opportunities that have added to the exposure of *Stripped Bare*. Thanks so much to Gary Johnson and blackmeninamerica.com for providing me with a national forum for getting my book and advice out to the masses. Brother, you move books! Thanks to the community of self-published authors who continue to support and inform me as I grow. Thanks to all of the small African American bookstores that took me on and supported my book—especially Karibu Books. Thanks to Victor Starr for taking a chance on me and giving me the radio gig that added to the credibility and reach of my book. Thanks to all of the publications and radio and television outlets, both local and national, that took the time to review and feature

Stripped Bare. All of you have contributed in some small way to getting me where I am today.

I am also lucky to have literary professionals in my corner who are patient and have worked closely with me to make sure this project gets off the ground. Thanks to Victoria Sanders for believing and being a truly informed source to help me make sense of this literary thing. Thanks to Melody Guy for supporting the book and answering all my crazy questions. My team is the best around.

Finally, I would like to thank all of my listeners and readers for enriching my writing experience. Thanks for opening a small window on your love experiences so that others could learn and grow. You are so brave to talk about the very issues we all deal with every day but choose to keep private out of fear and pride. Thanks for having the courage to pursue the best in love. I love you all.

Special thanks and love go out to my parents Lamont and Deborah Wray and to my partner in crime, my brother, Lamont Wray, Jr.

JB and Alec, my two very best black men, the greatest guys I have ever met—thanks for the support and patience as our lives continue to evolve. Love always and forever.

—LaDawn

CONTENTS

AUTHOR'S NOTE

In order to add sizzle to the text, I have incorporated many examples of romantic successes and failures. These stories do not reflect any one person in particular, but are broadly drawn stories used to clarify the text further. They are a compilation of stories I have heard, or lived, again and again.

So if you think I am writing about you, I'm not. Believe me, there is enough drama and passion in the world that it is definitely possible that if it has happened to me, it could indeed have happened to you.

So enjoy my many tales of love, and I hope these examples aid you in better understanding the truths.

INTRODUCTION

*W*elcome to a world of better relationships! Three years ago I came up with the idea of writing a series of relationship books for the African American community that would be based on twelve basic truths that can greatly improve the quality of love in our lives. These truths are tested—they have worked successfully for my sister circle and me—and I know that they can work for you. It is simply time for all sisters to have great relationships they deserve, with the very best black men!

Don't believe the hype. I am going to strip away the negative perceptions of black love that are sold to us every day. It is time to move forward and get the great relationship that is out there for you. From the truths you will gather practical ideas on how to actively pursue only the best relationships. Let go of the negative falsehoods. Live in reality and improve your relationships from day one!

I want you to pay close attention to the next sentence because it will revolutionize the way you view your relationship potential. *The key to a great relationship is you.* There are no tricks or steps that need to be followed—no special places to meet men, no magical weave or makeup that can guarantee a fulfilling partnership with a brother. What I am offering are basic, proven truths that allow us black women to foster the ultimate relationship with the very best black men. Get ready to jump into the driver's seat and enter a new territory where you consciously decide to have the best in your life without the concessions, drama, or dehumanization that other relationship guides offer. This book was written especially for you.

Using the truths will increase your ability to identify, pursue, and keep the very best black man. Each truth will reveal an aspect of personal development that will prepare you for living your best life. Living well and being self-fulfilled is contagious. Black men who are living their best lives will be drawn to your winning spirit. It is up to you to absorb the ideas behind the truths and run with them down the road toward personal fulfillment.

In talking with sister friends who have successfully reviewed and used the truths in their own relationships, I was always told that the truths deserved to be known outside of our little circle. So in the spirit of sisterhood, I am sharing the truths with you. They worked for me, and they will work for you. It is time to take charge of your romantic life and get the high-quality love that you deserve. Join me, sisters, as we pursue one of the world's greatest creations—black men.

All the best—

LaDawn Black

THAT'S THE TRUTH

I have been able to more clearly define

what I want and need in a relationship.

I no longer feel that I am not worthy

of the best love.

—Dana, 29

one

GUIDELINES FOR
THE TRUTHS

*A*re you ready to get stripped? It is time to let go of all of the misconceptions you have about black love and move into prosperous relationships that serve to feed your mind, body, and spirit. We are getting ready to call all of the news media, television shows, and women's magazines liars, because there *are* good black men out there who are still looking for great sisters to call their own. Our challenge is not with our men. The real challenge is reprogramming ourselves so that we can be contributors to our relationships, not detractors. The truths will revolutionize your approach to relationships.

WHY HAVE THE TRUTHS?

The state of relationships between brothers and sisters is on shaky ground. Everywhere you turn there are images of strong single black moms, black men with their nonblack wives, or black women hanging on to the worst possible men ever because they're afraid of being alone. If you tend to believe the media, sitcoms, and water cooler gossip, then you are probably feeling that there is little hope for finding the very best black man out there for you.

Play close attention, ladies: *there are many great black men out there.* Do not buy into the lies that all the good men are already married or gay. These are lies sold to our community so that we don't forge strong family or personal relationships, which have statistically proven to contribute to long, secure, and prosperous lives. Further, it is my belief that sisters clothe themselves with these lies so that we can justify our inability to select quality men or end bad relationships.

Our ability to have positive relationships is not completely shaped by insecure black men, our relationships with our fathers, socioeconomic conditions, or any other psychobabble that you have been sold in the past through the media and other relationship guides. These arguments do have some merit, but only you can decide to drop the negativity of the past and move forward into a better future. It is time to put the past away and live in the present—a present that is filled with new experiences and great love. The basic idea that I want you to open up your mind to today is that the very best black man is available to you. It is up to you to take the proactive steps to pursue and keep him.

Welcome to the best and most practical relationship advice that you will ever receive—advice that pushes you toward action and will not leave you lying in wait for the dream brother to discover you on that back pew, in the third cubicle from the left, or in the produce aisle. What I am offering is relationship truths that work not through deep psychoanalysis or childhood revelations but through identifying proactive behaviors that make you the master of your relationship destiny. Contrary to popular belief, the very best black men are not just out there somewhere waiting to discover you. You will have to be the aggressor, taking the steps to identify, pursue, and nurture a great relationship.

For all of the benefits that the truths will bring you, it is also important to note what they will not do. The truths will not:

- ❧ Change a bad brother into a good one
- ❧ Blame all of your bad relationship choices on Mommy or Daddy
- ❧ Tell you that there are not enough good black men out there
- ❧ Increase your net income, get you a Benz, or move you into a new house

If you desire any of the above, then this is not the book for you. We are digging a little deeper here and trying to undo a lot of the relationship behaviors and concepts that we black women have accepted in order to justify not having the love we deserve. In the end, the truths will provide you with ideas that will empower you to consciously decide to have the very best in your life.

A GOOD MAN?

What exactly do I mean when I say that the truths will result in you landing the very best black man? Are we talking about rich and highly educated brothers only? Let me clear this misconception up way ahead of time. We black women have fallen hard for the concept of a good man being a mucho provider and not much else. All of the other intangible characteristics that involve his ability to love and successfully partner and parent are viewed as gravy. We seem to latch on to "ballers" without giving any credence to the key attributes that contribute to successful relationships. Take inventory of those around you whose relationships you admire. I would say that the motivator in these relationships isn't money but friendship. When was the last time that you chose a best friend based on her bank account?

For my purposes the very best black man is one who is able to feed your spirit and body through compassion, understanding, dedication to goals, honesty, wit, and respect. The very best brother for you will be the one who is able to meet *all* of your needs—not just the superficial ones—even if you don't need him to.

WHERE DID THE TRUTHS
COME FROM?

So exactly how did I come up with the truths? Over seven years ago I made the decision to have better men in my life. My dating years up to that point were primarily filled with two types of brothers: the psychos and the bohos. Psychos are pretty self-explanatory. I have done my time with stalkers, criminals, weedheads, and mama's boys gone wild. The second group, the bohos, or misguided bohemians, includes the men who appear good on the outside but are either mind-numbingly boring or closeted sluts. To this day I don't know which group I found to be the most distasteful, but I do know that I decided I wanted and needed a change.

Late one night while doing my regular journal writing, I came up with what I considered the most critical traits for the very best black man for me. My wish list probably looked a lot like yours: loving, compassionate, good father material, goal-oriented, strong, sexy, passionate, and honest. This was my ideal man, and at the time I thought that all I had to do was keep this list in mind as I met brothers and I would automatically be able to identify the weeds and get rid of them. I did start meeting great brothers who were successful and by all accounts good men, but I was failing to forge deep connections. I was getting the first dates but not the long-term interest. Still trying to figure out the relationship game, I turned to those women in my circle who I felt had great black men in their lives. What was their secret? Where was I coming up short?

When I looked closer, it became clear to me that these relationships that I so respected were win-win arrangements. The brothers in these relationships were just as thankful and appreciative of their wives as their wives were of them. There was a balance—neither partner was responsible for the success of the relationship or burdened with its failings. I had been right in identifying what it was that I wanted in an ideal black man, but I was missing the other critical piece of the relationship equation: was I the ideal mate for the man that I was looking for? I began to look at what I could do to make myself the ideal partner for the man I was hoping to meet. What steps could I take to make my relationships work? It was after this thought process that the truths started to take form.

My discovery that night was that there were certain basic ideas governing personal interaction that, if absorbed, would lead women to identify the very best black men every time. Having identified them, sisters would be able to remain with these great men in mutually satisfying relationships. I placed these ideas into practice, and never again did I feel that I always attracted the wrong men or was not good enough to keep them. These ideas gave me the power to actively pursue great men and consistently be their top choice.

THE PLAN

Throughout this book I will share stories of how the truths have benefited sisters in identifying, pursuing, and nurturing great relationships with only the very best black men.

Each chapter focuses on one particular truth and ends with the lesson behind the truth. It is my hope that you will take both the truth and the lesson and add them to your arsenal of tools for improving your life. At the end of each chapter there is a "bare necessity," a term I chose to use instead of "affirmation." Affirmations, in my opinion, are pleasant thoughts that dwell in the background, while bare necessities call on you to take action today—and it is only through action that change can occur. If a particular truth really hits home, I would suggest that you highlight the bare necessity. For your convenience, at the end of the book I have added a cheat sheet for both the truths and the bare necessities so that you can easily rip them out of the book and carry them with you to reflect on. It is only through examining and thinking about a truth that it can become integrated in your everyday behavior.

It is key that the truths be taken and absorbed as basic ideas for living, not as a check-off list for romantic behavior. These ideas work to improve you—not frazzle you into completing idiotic tasks, challenges, and lists on the road to love. The formula is simple. Use the truths to improve you. An improved sense of self will then lead to a more fulfilling love life.

So sit in your favorite chair or get wrapped up in your thickest throw, relax, and open your mind to the truths. I promise that once you have soaked up the ideas and lessons, you will see that the key to getting the very best black man is you. The truths are here to make sure that you are being the very best you can be as you pursue the very best black man.

Let's go!

TRUTH I
LET GO OF THE PAST

Letting go of the idea that all men lie

is hard for me.

—Tracey, 34

LaDawn,

I am involved with a great brother who loves me and treats me like a queen. However, I stay in his ass about his seeing other women. Now, he hasn't done anything to deserve this, but every man I have ever been involved with has cheated on me. How can I learn to give this brother a chance? I really do want to be happy.

You are dealing with some heavy baggage wrapped around what brothers have done to you in the past. Why are you holding on to that stuff? You clearly have a brother in your life who is worthy of trust. Stop wasting your energy looking around corners, checking his wallet (I know you are doing it ☺), and stressing over when he will leave. While you are doing all this, you are missing out on quality time with a great brother. Let go of all the stuff that other brothers have done to you and focus on what your man is doing right now.

Now, don't turn into a fool. Hold on to the lessons of past loves, but learn to differentiate between a life lesson and baggage. Learn the lesson and apply it to your future decisions, but leave the hurt and regret behind you because they stand in the way of being happy and complete right now.

————

two

PUT YOUR BAGS
DOWN AND
GET COMFORTABLE

*M*y name is LaDawn Black, and I have baggage. Unlike most sisters, I can be up front and say that I have had issues with men who lie, have bad teeth, are unmotivated, live with their mommas, cry a whole lot, speak broken English, look better than me, always seem to need a haircut, have any type of body odor, or are over 6 feet and 250 pounds (I have a strong phobia of being crushed). These are the things that I took into consideration when I met a man, even in a casual situation—I'd begin to protect myself immediately. My justification was that life was too short to keep making the same mistakes.

After spending a few years ducking about 60 percent of the available brothers, I decided to lighten my load. I realized that I was greatly limiting the amount of love in my life by judging new brothers on others' mistakes. If I wanted to meet the man of my dreams, I had to let my prior experiences go and be open to new possibilities.

Truth I opened my eyes to how I was standing in my own way when it came to hooking up with a great brother. I made the decision to stop judging and start learning. Just because the food is in a familiar package doesn't mean that it will always taste the same. Drop the baggage from the past and sample a new and exciting flavor!

❧ TRUTH I

LET GO OF THE PAST

Holding on to the past will destroy your present situation. Instead of enjoying a new experience and growing, you will be constantly on the lookout for clues to your relationship's imminent demise.

Too many times we quickly sum up new people in our lives based on our prior experiences with people who were similar to them. It is so easy to do, and I will admit that I have done it on many occasions. In making these snap judgments, though, we miss the true essence of the person right in front of us.

How many times have we told ourselves that we will never be that dumb again? To this day I think about some of the relationship situations that I was in and wonder how in the world I survived. So like all the other sisters out there, I sucked up the lesson and stomped through future relationships vowing to never again deal with a liar, cheater, or anyone who made his living as a children's clown (sad but true).

On the surface, this dedication to moving forward appeared to be productive. I did what we are all taught to do: I identified the problem and took positive steps so that it would never occur again—case closed. Well, in an ideal world this would be the end of the matter, but you know as well as I do that the past has a tendency not to stay in the past, and often past relationship hurts play a major role in the current relationship's health.

Many times we are so busy worrying about what our current love interest will do to us that we miss all of the wonderful things that our lovers are doing. Let's take my girlfriend Tracey, for instance. Tracey is 34 years old and is looking to find a great companion. Her career as a political fund-raiser allows her to attend all of Washington, D.C.'s hottest political soirées, and Tracey would love to have someone to share the parties with. In the past she has always dated brothers who are very similar to her: highly educated, career-driven, and politically connected. On the surface these men are ideal for Tracey, because she doesn't want to get married and she's looking for a man who can carry his own weight both financially and socially.

TRACEY AND KWAME

One hot August night at a co-worker's barbecue Tracey met Kwame, a 36-year-old senatorial aide from Alabama. Not only is Kwame absolutely milk-chocolate gorgeous, but he is also just as politically connected and career-savvy as Tracey. That night these two sizzling politicos pulled out their PDAs and agreed that a second meeting was definitely in order.

After dating for three months, Tracey and Kwame had hit that comfortable mode when you are calling anytime and stopping by your lover's place at the drop of a hat. One day when Kwame was on his way back to D.C. from spending Thanksgiving at his parents' house in Alabama, Tracey decided to set up the ultimate surprise welcome-back party. She rushed over to Kwame's place with the works in hand: flowers, candles, incense, a Luther Vandross CD, and her most wicked red lace nightie. Tracey let herself into his place and went about setting up the apartment for her very private party.

With only a half hour left before Kwame arrived home, Tracey ran into the bathroom to shower and change into her wicked number. After her shower Tracey retrieved her travel bag from the bathroom floor and quickly discovered that she had run out of toothpaste. "No problem," she thought, "I'll use Kwame's." She looked on the counter, but there was no toothpaste in sight. Tracey then opened Kwame's medicine cabinet and still could not find a tube. Feeling desperate, she remembered that he kept his gym bag on the floor of his bedroom closet. There had to be some toothpaste in there.

Quickly Tracey retrieved Kwame's toiletry bag and ran back into the bathroom. She found the toothpaste, but then a small prescription bottle caught her eye. Tracey removed the bottle from the bag and flipped it over to look at the label. The bottle contained a common drug to treat herpes—Tracey had seen numerous commercials for it on TV. How could this be happening to her again?

When Tracey and Kwame first met, she had been brutally honest about her past with Trevor, which ended abruptly with her being treated for an STD. She made it very clear to Kwame before they were first intimate that she wanted him to have a clean bill of health. And she told him in no uncertain terms that to be her lover he had to be monogamous. She'd been burned in her past relationship and did not find out that she had an STD until the other woman called Tracey at her office to tell her.

Kwame had assured Tracey that he was perfectly healthy. He had even gone so far as to send a small ice cream cake to her job that said simply "A OK, some please." Tracey was charmed and jumped into the next phase of their relationship without any second thoughts. But this prescription bottle was a sign, and she would not ignore it the way she had with Trevor, who had been able to explain away his mystery scratches and sudden interest in weekend trips with his college buddies. Tracey was not going to allow Kwame to simply explain away this pill bottle.

So when Kwame walked through the door, instead of being pleasantly surprised by the scent of the incense and the soft candlelight, a furious Tracey caught him off guard. Tracey threw the pill bottle at Kwame's head and stomped into the bedroom to put on her clothes.

Retrieving the pill bottle from his feet, Kwane quickly realized why she was furious. He turned to walk into the bedroom to talk to Tracey but was nearly run over as she headed toward the door.

Kwame grabbed Tracey's shoulder and pleaded with her to sit down and hear him out. Tracey quickly removed his hand from her shoulder and informed him that there was nothing for them to discuss. But as she was about to leave she turned around and said, "One question—are they your pills?" Kwame said, "Yes and no." That was the last straw—Tracey threw her overnight bag at Kwame's chest.

Kwame managed to deflect the bag, but its contents spilled out onto his porch. Tracey, blind with anger and hurt, stooped down to pick up her things at the same time Kwame bent down to help her, and their heads nearly collided. Kwame began to explain that the pills were in his name but that they were actually for his little brother, Kelvin, who was too embarrassed to go with their mom to the doctor.

Kelvin knew that he had been exposed to herpes through his girlfriend and had asked Kwame to get the prescription for him and to bring it down this weekend. Kwame's friend Mike, a doctor, had written the prescription up for him. Kwame knew it was wrong to get the fake prescription, but he also knew what it felt like to be a 16-year-old boy still going to the doctor's office with your mom. When Mike gave him the pills, he transferred them into another bottle and thought he had thrown the original away.

Tracey didn't know what to do. Should she believe this story and go back into Kwame's place, or should she just break it off now because even if he wasn't lying this time, don't all men eventually lie? Kwame had never ever lied to her before. Once he had actually tried to lie to her about working late at the office, but later in the day he'd called her to tell her that he really wasn't going to be working late—he was going to the mall to pick out her birthday present.

As Tracey placed the last items in her bag, Kwame mentioned that if he were trying to keep something away from her, he definitely wouldn't keep it in his gym bag. He knew for a fact that she raided his toiletry bag on the regular for disposable razors. He laughed and said, "You didn't notice that I switched to the pink kind with a moisture strip? That was not a change for this face." At this Tracey had to laugh. She basically lived out of Kwame's gym bag, and she thought he had switched to the pink razors because they were cheaper. Kwame wouldn't lie to her, she realized, and Tracey had to pick up her face and go back in the house. Thinking about the night she had planned, she thought, "What good's a party without a hostess?"

THE LOWDOWN

Sisters, we have the tendency to measure every man we meet by the men we have dealt with in the past. We assume all light-skinned men think they are cute, blue-collar men don't have any money, churchgoing men are the best! All of your assumptions may possess a small amount of truth, but they are never true in all cases.

When you first meet a man, judge him on his own merits. Allow him to succeed as your partner based on his actions and not on your preconceived notions. I guarantee you that you will find that both your positive and negative experiences in the past will be of little consequence to your future.

Sisters, you just don't know how many brothers have told me how excited they were about meeting a sister only to have her launch into bad stories about her exes or go on and on about the great one who got away. These types of remembrances from the past drain the energy from new relationships. Just think when was the last time a man endeared himself to you by talking about how wonderful his ex was.

❧ TRUTHFUL LESSON

Let the present dictate present conditions.

Allow yourself to live in the present, and let all past experiences—both positive and negative—go. Nobody wants to constantly bump up against the past when trying to forge a relationship for the future. Not that I am telling you to become gullible or a fool. You do need to know when a man is lying to you or working contrary to your best interests. What I am saying is to base judgments on the very best man's actions and not the prior behavior of duds. Living in the past is the quickest way to never have a fulfilling future.

❧ BARE NECESSITY

I WILL TAKE TODAY ON ITS OWN MERITS.

TRUTH II
GAIN A SENSE OF FUN

Where are the men with a sense of adventure?

I can't do dinner and a movie all the time.

—*Kida, 22*

LaDawn,

What do you do when a man wants to do things that you have absolutely no interest in? My man loves gambling and the Vegas thing, but I find it all a bit wasteful and gaudy. I want to like what he likes, but sometimes love is just not enough.

Relationships have a real funny way of making us all look like liars. When you first hooked up with this brother, you were probably a Vegas nut just to be around him and keep his attention. Now that you are more comfortable in the relationship, you no longer feel like playing the role. Well, sis, you are going to have to keep it going by remaining fun and being open to new and different ways to spend time with your man.

Don't become a stick-in-the-mud, because that isn't what he fell in love with. Stay the hot and fun chick that he has grown to love.

three

JUST A DULL GIRL

This year I reinvented myself as Wonder Sister. On our annual vacation to the Bahamas I decided to try parasailing for the first time. The two prior summers, from the safety of my beach chair I'd criticized the crazed individuals who voluntarily soared through the air over a large body of water with what appeared to be little more than a blanket guiding the way. Inside, however, I was envious of the crazy folk because they had the courage to try a once-in-a-lifetime experience. It was time for me to get off the pot. As the wind whipped through my hair and the scenery around me fed my soul, I was reborn. Fun and adventure were still possible for me, and the taste of salt air had never been sweeter.

I love to have fun, and one of the best ways to do this is to try something new. Whether you're successful at it or you literally fall on your face trying, at least you can say that for a moment you stepped out of your comfort zone and were brazen enough to be one of the wild ones.

One time I remember being asked by the latest hot brother to compete with him in a couples' relay. A couples' relay is when a group of ten couples get together and go through a series of physical challenges that include things such as potato-sack racing, horseshoes, and other silly physical activities, with the losing team having to pay for a highly expensive dinner for the group. When the brother presented this idea, I was *so* not interested. I am by no means an athlete—volleyball was my nemesis growing up—so any suggestion that I would willingly participate in a physical challenge was totally ridiculous.

As I positioned myself to say no thanks to this offer, I had a eureka moment. In the past this brother had been gracious enough to sit through every foreign film that I dragged him to, and he had actually suggested that we go backstage after a musical to meet the cast and crew, so how could I not at least try this couples' relay? I knew full well that he didn't always enjoy my activities, but he was willing to try them in order to make me happy. It was time to reciprocate.

But even more important, how long was I going to continue limiting my experiences in life? Somehow along the way I had lost the courage to try something new. Who knew—maybe I would actually have fun. I decided to say yes to the couples' relay and get on with living. And you know what? I learned something important about myself that afternoon—not much has changed since gym class.

But I did have fun and was able to prove to a great brother that I was willing to step outside my comfort zone and do something different.

ARTIS

I remember one brother that I worked with several years ago by the name of Artis who was always going off on some great weekend adventure. One week it was whitewater rafting, another week rock climbing, and yet another week he would be flying to Vegas. Every Monday all of Artis' co-workers would be captivated by his stories about his travels and how surprised his latest lady was about their adventure.

For the multitude of great dates that Artis planned, very rarely did you hear the same woman's name mentioned for more than a few months. This was surprising to me because Artis was an intelligent and attractive 25-year-old brother who should have been able to woo and keep any woman. One day I asked Artis why he hadn't been able to find one special sister to share his adventures. His answer tied in perfectly to Truth II—gaining a sense of fun.

Artis told me a story that I had heard from many brothers about sisters sometimes forgetting how to simply have fun. He said, "Sisters get overly concerned with how activities may affect their hair, makeup, and nails, or they deem activities dumb or boring." In many ways Artis felt that sisters had "let go of the basic idea that new experiences enhance your quality of life."

He also made the point that he had encountered numerous sisters who were up for every adventure when they

first met him, but after a few months, when the sisters be-
lieved that the relationship was more solid, they felt freer
to call his interests boring or silly. It appeared that they
wanted to go back to the mainstay of dinner and a movie,
which Artis did not think was a bad date, but definitely not
the level of excitement that he wanted to have around him
in the long term.

In Artis' mind, there were many great sisters he wanted
to be with who in the end just were not creative or ener-
getic enough to want to invest in keeping the relationship
fun and fresh. Therefore, every few months Artis would try
to strike an excitement chord with a new sister in the hope
that she would finally be the one.

❧ TRUTH II

GAIN A SENSE OF FUN

Be open to new experiences and remain creative and sponta-
neous. Create the excitement that you want out of life.

THE LOWDOWN

Remember the times when you could just go for a walk
with a guy and have fun thinking of new things to do on
your next cheap date? Poor dates were often the best dates
because you had to be creative in order to have fun, and
you cherished the time together because it was always such
a unique experience. One of my best dates actually took
place at a Laundromat because we wanted to see each
other but both had laundry to do.

In today's atmosphere of full schedules and immediate gratification there is little time for simply sitting back and having a shared experience with another. We are the generation of planned fun—which often comes with an agenda and a hefty price tag. When was the last time that you had a conversation so good that you actually forgot what time it was? Can you even recall the last time that you went somewhere and had the most fun you've ever had in your life? It is time to journey back to the era of amusement parks, house parties, and walks in the park. It is time to reconnect to fun.

Gaining a sense of fun is critical, sisters, in that a sense of adventure and initiative is extremely attractive. Oftentimes when we meet a great brother we are up for everything he suggests, from hiking in the mountains to learning to salsa, but when he asks us what we want to do, we can't come up with a thing. This is frustrating for brothers because they want someone who has her own interests and who can carry her own weight in terms of keeping the relationship fresh and relevant.

KIDA

One example of a sister who lives up to the challenge of keeping a relationship fun is my girlfriend Kida. Kida is a 22-year-old recent college graduate who is working her way up in public relations. In addition to working full-time she is also attending graduate school at night. Kida is extremely busy and can't tolerate the idea of even being friends with a brother who isn't at least half as busy as she is. To hear Kida say it, she needs a guy with plans—she has no time for the routine.

At lunch one day we were talking about what dating was like for her, and she quickly mentioned that she couldn't deal with boring men. If all a brother can come up with is going to the movies, then he definitely is not the man for her. "There are too many things that you can do for free rather than spend another $10 at the movies," Kida said. She's constantly looking for new things to do, and if a guy isn't interested in at least trying something new, than she knows she has to move on. "The way a brother starts out with you is the way he is going to end up," Kida told me. "I like to have fun, and I want him to want to have fun as well."

The other thing that we sisters do is switch up once we feel more secure in a relationship and decide that we are no longer interested in doing particular things. We feel that he really likes us now; therefore we no longer have to feign interest in things that were never quite that interesting to us in the first place, like sports, jazz, or his job. At this point we have no problem telling the very best black man that his interests are lame, boring, or plain stupid.

Now, when you tell your man that you have always found particular activities or interests of his boring, he feels that you two do not have as much in common as he once thought. Even worse, he now knows that you have lied to him. There are only two ways to remedy this situation. Either you remain quiet and keep doing things that you hate to do or you stop doing them and watch your relationship slowly unravel.

❦ TRUTHFUL LESSON

> *Go for the unexpected. Open yourself up to adventure.*

Ladies, ignoring Truth II can be a relationship-killer. Once the relationship is no longer fun, one or both parties will start to seek enjoyment elsewhere. The key to Truth II is that a sense of adventure and the spirit to do new things are very attractive. When you have your own interests and are constantly looking to have new experiences, you are letting that very best black man know that you can hold up your end in keeping a relationship fresh. No one wants to carry the entire relationship. Take responsibility for keeping yourself fun and interesting. If you do, everyone will want to join the party!

❦ BARE NECESSITY

TODAY I WILL TRY SOMETHING NEW.

TRUTH III
MAKE YOUR
RELATIONSHIP
A TOP PRIORITY

We cut off our phones and spend as much time

as we can alone. No one outside the relationship

gets a say during Derek and Jonese time.

—*Jonese, 35*

LaDawn,

I have been married for fifteen years to a great man. Throughout our marriage he has proven to me that he is a great provider, partner, and parent. So what can I do to add a little spice to our relationship? We have been on cruise control the last few years, and I hunger for the passion-filled days from early in our relationship.

You are suffering from the relationship blahs, which affect so many relationships after several years of more of the same. You want to get back to the place where you guys were when you first met, but you have to realize that you will never experience that first blush of love again. That time in your life was special because all things were new and there were none of the distractions that come with making a life together, such as kids, careers, and bills. However, there is one thing that you can take from your early years, and that is the thought and effort that you devoted to impressing each other.

Early in relationships we all want to knock the socks off our partner, so we are constantly thinking of new ways to excite and entice him. After a few years together we stop doing that. Make your relationship a top priority, and once again you will be thinking of creative ways to keep your husband enthralled. Let him in on this secret, and he will start to surprise you again as well. What's needed is a simple priority shuffle—not a relationship overhaul.

four

⁂

GET STINGY

$\mathcal{G}$et stingy when it comes to your love life. This is one of my favorite truths because this one will make your relationships sing. Make the one you're with feel that there is no other person in the world who comes before him and that your relationship is more important than any other.

I am incredibly stingy when it comes to my relationship because I realize that in the end, when all of the friends, family, careers, and children have gone away, the only person you will be left with is your partner. With my husband there are guidelines that we follow to make sure our relationship takes priority. We call them the Black Commandments. Here's a small sample:

We shall not socialize separately.

Let's get the gossip at the same time.

We shall not answer the phone in the evening.

Is your house so boring that you have to call ours?

We shall not have guests over the house without the other present.

This one is more for me. My husband does all of the cooking. Why inconvenience myself?

We shall never discuss our disagreements outside of the home.

We would lose the respect of our friends and family if we told them about our fight over the last piece of popcorn shrimp.

Although our guidelines appear silly on the surface, they do go a long way in making sure that we set boundaries for the amount of input others have in our relationship. By taking on these selfish attitudes and activities, we are able to make sure that we are feeding the needs of our relationship first, which results in each of us having a better relationship experience.

Giving your relationship priority reinforces the core of the relationship and quickly lets others know that there is no room to tamper in this great thing. I love Truth III because it can improve your love life on so many levels as you learn that the only people who ever truly care about the success of your relationship are the people who are in it!

❧ TRUTH III

MAKE YOUR RELATIONSHIP
A TOP PRIORITY

You two come first. All others are second.

THE LOWDOWN

From day one keep the confidences of your lover and work out relationship issues within the relationship. Do not allow outside forces to leapfrog your relationship needs, because if you start this practice you will never be able to stop it. A lot of relationships have died because sisters have let their girlfriends or mom in on relationship issues only to have them escalate a minor concern to a level that you know it never would have reached otherwise. Maintain the integrity of your relationship by keeping confidences.

Now, I know this is hard for sisters to do because we feel that our decisions on some level can be made easier by having others' input, but this practice never ever works. Just think how many times a girlfriend of yours asked your "honest opinion" of her man and you gave it, only to have her either go tell him about it (he can't stand you now) or start an argument with you for thinking so negatively about her man. How many times have you witnessed good families ruined because they have divided their support for a couple? To this day we have couples in our families where only one member of the couple is allowed to show up for gatherings because relationship issues have made their way out into the familial community. At times you can even catch heat for being positive about your girl's relationship because she takes your encouragement as possible interest in her guy—and we all know how badly this can turn out.

The rule is that even with the closest of girlfriends and family it is best to keep your relationship and its happenings off-limits. Believe me, those who love you will be there for you in time of need regardless of whether or not they know the blow-by-blow history of your relationship.

JONESE AND DEREK

My girlfriend Jonese learned this truth recently when she was trying to decide whether or not to move in with her boyfriend, Derek. Derek and Jonese had been going out for eight months, and Jonese stayed at Derek's condo most of the week. When Jonese decided to go back to school full-time to finish her degree, Derek suggested that instead of weighing herself down with loans, she should give up her apartment and just move in with him. His belief was that she pretty much lived with him anyway and this was just the next logical step.

Jonese was confused as to what to do. She loved Derek and things were going great for them as a couple, but did she want to give up her freedom and move in with a man who was not her husband? If she said no to Derek, would he think Jonese didn't value their relationship as much as he did? Should she just move in with the man she loved and be happy that he was in a position to ease things for her financially? Jonese was going in circles.

She thought to call her mom for advice but knew that her mom would just go into her routine about sin and how Jonese was already sleeping with the man and now she was going to compound the sin by moving in. Jonese then thought about asking her girl Dinah her opinion, but realized that Dinah loved Derek like a little brother and would encourage Jonese to burn her eyebrows off if it guaranteed that Dinah could one day be a bridesmaid. The only other person Jonese thought she could probably consult was her girl Shelley. Shelley would be objective and tell Jonese what she thought she should do, but Shelley sometimes would rub it in if you went against her advice and the situation went bad. Jonese knew that she couldn't deal with that pressure.

After thinking about it for a few days, Jonese decided that all the well-meaning advice in the world would not do her any good. This decision was about her life, and she was the only one who had to live with its consequences. She and Derek had a very detailed conversation over dinner one night to discuss the possibility of her moving in. After their conversation Jonese decided that although she loved Derek and appreciated his generous offer, she was not ready to give up her financial independence. They agreed that they would see how her first semester went. If things got hard for Jonese financially, they would talk again about possibly moving in together. By being stingy and keeping this issue within the relationship, Jonese was able to make a clear decision based on what she needed and not others' opinions. No one in Jonese and Derek's circle was privy to or able to pass judgment on a major relationship step that in the end did not even occur.

Another aspect of getting stingy is to avoid letting out-side forces crowd your relationship. When you are with your man turn the phone and television off. Take a few moments to truly listen and respond to what he says. Do not allow others to move in on your time together. If you value your relationship this way, others will as well.

Crowding is a huge issue because sometimes we can schedule and obligate ourselves out of relationship suc-cess. It is critical that you place your needs as a couple first, over any outside obligations. When you first met you had all the time and attention in the world for your lover; why should this change? Get stingy and let others know that the weekends and evenings are your time with your man. You will be amazed at how careful people will be when they approach you. You will no longer be the prime target of the time wasters and favor seekers who look to take away valu-able time from nurturing the love in your life.

TABITHA

This crowding issue is big for my girl Tabitha, but with a twist. She has told all of us on many occasions that she does not answer her phone after 7 p.m. For years we thought that she was strange and just being difficult, but this was not the case. Tabitha is a single mother of one who feels that if she does not set this guideline with friends and fam-ily, she will be drained by the time she goes to bed. Being stingy with her time has helped Tabitha reinforce her top relationship—her relationship with herself.

❦ TRUTHFUL LESSON

Nothing should dull the luster of your relationship. Others complement the relationship; they are not the core.

No matter what the nature of the relationship, if you place a high regard on it others will also. By prioritizing your commitments and making it clear to everyone that your relationship takes priority over all others, you will find that you will no longer be held captive by others. It is time to get stingy!

❦ BARE NECESSITY

I WILL GIVE MYSELF SPACE.

TRUTH IV
SEX IS NOT A
FOUR-LETTER WORD

Men are freaky. Why should I do everything for him

when he is not willing to do even the basics for me?

—*Janet, 41*

LaDawn,

I am a normal brother who believes that I am a good lover. Currently I am dating a lady who is beautiful and sexy, but she will not make love during the day or with the lights on. I constantly tell her that she is beautiful, but this seems not to do a damn thing. What can I do to get this very special woman to open up and love a brother in the light?

There are so many negative messages about black women's beauty out there that it isn't a stretch that your lady may feel that her body does not fit the ideal. If you add to this that many little girls are still being raised to believe that their sexuality and sexual urges are dirty, then it is a miracle that many sisters even make it to the bedroom at all, let alone allow a brother to explore their bodies with the lights on.

You should be applauded for your effort and patience in trying to convince your lady of her sex appeal and desirability, but you may want to try this as well. Why not work the sister up to love in the light by first introducing candles in the bedroom? Candlelight is soft and flattering to everyone. Next you may want to suggest making love during the day in a steamy bathroom. The steam will provide a slight sexy veil for the sister while you get to see and experience pretty much everything. The key is to ease her into her sexual comfort zone and understand where her insecurities come from.

five

LOVE SUCKS SOMETIMES

I love sex! I was blessed with a healthy sense of my own sexuality and a keen openness to what others view as hot. Not only is sex one of the greatest experiences on earth, but it is also a guaranteed conversation starter. Over the years these conversations moved through "What is sex like?" to "Do you do it?" to "Are you still doing it?" At each stage the conversations have been enlightening, delving into length, stamina, and how long it's been since the great one. This entire dialog is great, but I have noticed a slight change in the way sisters now choose to talk about their sexuality.

I will never forget a recent gathering with some sisters where we got on the topic of sex. I was amazed by how frankly and easily these sisters were able to say that they don't like having sex with their men and that they don't do certain sexual acts anymore because they are married and no longer have to. This totally blew my mind because these were gorgeous sisters who would rather complain to their girls about the sex they get than work out the issue with their men.

Sisters, when did it become okay to publicize the fact that you are not giving your man any? If your man is so repulsive, why are you still with him? Could the problem in our sex lives be us? Is it possible that we haven't had the good stuff, therefore we really don't think we are missing all that much?

Look, I know more than anyone that a sister can get busy sometimes and that when this happens the last thing on your mind is having sex or being sexy. I remember one time being in the mix of graduate school, work, and writing and being asked by my husband to meet him at a romantic restaurant for a special dinner. At 8 p.m. sharp I showed up at this beautiful restaurant in jeans, tennis shoes, and a backpack. As I waited for my husband to arrive I mentally justified my ridiculous choice of dress as being appropriate for the cold weather and sensible because I had to walk six blocks from the subway, plus I had just gotten out of class—what did he expect? Later, when my husband showed up, he complimented me on my sexy earmuffs and choice of cherry lip balm. What else could the brother say? Sometimes even I need a truth refresher!

I was trying to justify my lack of zest and sexual verve regarding the evening, but the fact was that I just did not take the time to be sexy. I was overwhelmed and ignoring

my sexual self. I had successfully turned what was supposed to be a very special evening into an average one.
This never would have happened when we were dating. I
would have changed clothes on the subway platform during rush hour if it meant that I got to spend a half hour with
this great guy.

Now is the time to reconnect to our sexual selves. It is
time to closely examine our attitudes regarding our sexuality and make peace with them. Stop blaming brothers for
your sexual energy and appetites and take a lead role in discovering your pleasures and enhancing his. If you are not
comfortable in your sexuality, then there is no way that you
can come together with a brother and please him. Further,
if you don't know what is pleasing to you, how can you ever
hope to let the brother in your life know how to get it right?

❧ TRUTH IV

SEX IS NOT A FOUR-LETTER WORD

Know what pleases you sexually and tell your man how to do it.
Ask him what he needs and give it to him.

THE LOWDOWN

In the interest of attracting and keeping a quality black
man, we have to shake up our prevailing attitudes toward
sex to make sure that we are in touch constantly with what
we need and what it takes to keep a man happy. The very
best black man is looking for someone who is comfortable
with her sexuality in such a way that she can both accurately

tell him how to please her and be open to him telling her how to please him. Without this two-way communication your sex life will die off over the duration of the relationship.

MYA AND STEVE

My girl Mya relayed a story to me that ties into Truth IV. She and her husband, Steve, had been married for four years, and whenever they were flipping through the channels late at night looking for something to watch, Steve always stopped on the adult video channels and jokingly asked Mya if she wanted to buy a movie. This was funny maybe the first two times that Steve did it, but now Mya was quietly bothered by Steve's "joke."

Porn was not repulsive to Mya. She thought that it definitely could enhance a couple's sexual experience, but she felt that Steve wanted it for a different reason—to point out to Mya what she could be doing better. Steve and Mya, for all their similarities, are glaringly different in one area: Steve has had a great deal of sexual experience, while Mya has had only two sexual partners. She has always felt that she didn't quite know enough to please him, and she viewed his suggestions to buy films as his way of nicely telling her that she needed to learn some new tricks.

Mya suffered in silence for a few months, because how could she tell Steve that he was making her insecure? Finally tiring of the "joke," Mya asked Steve why he was always asking her about buying porn. In order not to seem so desperate, she thought she would flip it onto him by asking him if he needed it to improve his skills.

To her surprise, Mya learned from Steve that it wasn't that either of them needed a crash course. He thought their sex life was great and hoped that she was pleased too. Steve just thought that watching a movie together would be a different experience, not unlike the whipped cream and chocolate undies they had tried months before. He wasn't looking for her to get it right—just to enhance their mutual experience.

In the same way we constantly try to stay current on fashion, business, and political trends, we need to stay plugged into what the very best black man may find attractive. When was the last time you saw a movie, watched a video, or perused the newsstand to determine what the new look is? Are there ways that you can incorporate these looks? What are the hot topics that men are discussing? What type of image is being sold to our men as ideal? This is crucial information for any woman because only the informed sister will know how to attract and keep the very best man interested sexually.

Now, don't get defensive. I am not saying that you have to turn into a video ho in order to attract and keep a brother. I am in agreement with you that a lot of the images of black women in the media are inappropriate and highly sexualized and don't reflect what most of us value and want. But what I am trying to say is that our men are catching glimpses of these images every day, and consciously or not, they are forming opinions about what appeals to them personally. Why not plug in to what men find sexy? Show them that reality beats a video or magazine any day!

CELIA AND HAKIM

Celia is a 35-year-old procurement manager whom I have known since grade school. Ever since I first met Celia she has always worn her hair long. Celia's family is very traditional. Girls are supposed to look like girls, and boys are supposed to look like boys. Women in Celia's family do not cut their hair short—ever.

As Celia got older and started climbing the career ladder she felt that her long hair served her well in reinforcing her professional image; however, on the personal side she started to feel that she was not looking her best. One night she was sitting with her fiancé, Hakim, watching television and Hakim commented that he liked the new thing that an actress was doing with her hair. Celia casually nodded and continued watching the program. Hakim then said, "You know, you would look great with that cut."

At that Celia took a closer look at the television and said, "Really? You think so? I always thought you liked my hair long."

"Yeah, I do," said Hakim, "but I think you would really look hot with short hair too. Besides, you are prettier than her anyway."

Celia smiled to herself and thought, "This man knows flattery will get him everywhere."

The very next week Celia went to her stylist with the latest *Essence* magazine in hand and asked him to make her a short-hair diva.

When I asked Celia about cutting her hair weeks later, I was really curious if she had done it only to feed Hakim's fantasy. She quickly said, "Yes and no." As his woman, she constantly felt the need to keep him interested in her, so if he suggested a color of underwear he'd like to see or that she wear her hair a certain way, she'd be more than willing to do it to make him happy. But cutting her hair was mostly for her. Celia and Hakim's sex life was great, but she realized she'd been starting to hold back a little because she was feeling a little run-down and stale. Why not shake up things a bit with a new style? It was time to be the sexiest Celia could be for Celia.

Looks weigh heavily in sexuality but by far are not the only consideration. Many of us sisters need to fess up and be honest about what turns us on and what doesn't. Sisters are carrying too much baggage from religion, our parents, the media, and bad men that tell us we are shortchanging ourselves in an area that it is only natural to enjoy. Take the time to ascertain what you like sexually. Be brave and tell the man in your life what you need. If he is not doing something correctly, let him know how he can make you feel better. So many times we will get with our girlfriends to say what a brother does wrong, but we have never gotten up the courage to tell the brother directly. So off he goes disrupting the world of the next sister. Men operate from a sense of knowing. Believe me, any great brother wants to know how he can please you.

Once you have schooled him on how to please you, focus on what it is that he needs. Guys are sometimes shy when it comes to telling you exactly what they need sexually. Most brothers will hint around or tug and pull at you to get you where they want you to be. The best way to determine what he needs is simply to ask. While watching a steamy film, ask if a particular move is something that he thinks is sexy. When you're out to dinner, ask him what his wildest time was and what his worst time was, and be open to his answers. Take the time to answer his questions as well. Sexual satisfaction comes from the free exchange of pleasures and turnoffs. Be open to his desires and change your game plan to reflect what you need and what your boundaries allow. Men are drawn to women who are comfortable in their sexual identity, whether it is the wild woman swinging from the chandelier or the closet freak.

Discovering who we are sexually takes some time and also takes a shake-up of what we as sisters consider permissible (kissing, fondling, missionary position) versus acts that no good girl is supposed to do (oral sex, anal sex, group sex). Where do we get these ideas? Why do we let forces outside ourselves determine our sexual boundaries? News flash, ladies: *there are no good or bad sexual acts*. There is just a huge menu that you can pick and choose from. Be open to sampling the menu, and communicate to your man that you are open to hearing his menu options as well. Be clear about your boundaries and be open to new pleasures.

JANET

Janet shared with me a story a few days ago that clearly drives home this point. Janet is a 41-year-old mother of a college freshman who is rediscovering after nearly twenty years what it is like to be a single sister. Our sister circle is riveted by her stories of trying to meet a great brother who is interested in an older woman looking to jump-start the next phase of her life. Janet is one of those incredibly attractive sisters who catch brothers off guard when she tells them that she has an adult son. Janet had hoped that her status as a single woman with no kids at home would make her very attractive to older brothers looking to live life to its fullest, but what she found was that these men just were not all that adventurous when it came to meeting her sexual needs.

In Janet's opinion most of the men she met were scared off by her energy and sexual frankness. She began to feel that maybe she should tone down some of her sexual opinions and play it cool with new men, but she realized that the men who were uncomfortable with her conversation wouldn't be a good fit for her sexually down the road. The way Janet sees it is that it's better to scare off a few with your clothes on than to lie frustrated with your clothes off.

❧ TRUTHFUL LESSON

Do what excites you . . . learn what excites him.

Make your sexual needs known to any man you are considering being intimate with. The key to a healthy view of sexuality is to be open to new experiences and honest about your boundaries. Keeping your sexuality thriving aids you in staying connected to your lover. Someone who is sexually pent up is a turnoff because there truly is no way to come together. Relationships are sparked by attraction, but they are reborn every day through communication. One of the strongest ways to communicate is through linking your body harmoniously with a great brother.

❧ BARE NECESSITY

I AM RESPONSIBLE FOR MY ULTIMATE PLEASURE.

TRUTH V
GET THE CLUES

Marco was always kidding that I did not listen

to him. One day I stopped and actually focused

on what he had been saying to me, and I was

shocked at what I discovered.

—*Georgia, 37*

————————

LaDawn,

I listen to your show every night and I need some advice. Should I leave my man? He has women calling our phone at all hours of the night, he disappears for days, and I can't remember the last time he contributed to the household bills. I am starting to think he may have someone else. I love him, but I am confused.

What do you not get?

————————

six

MY GOODNESS, OPEN YOUR EYES

I am a super sleuth. When I was dating I was constantly looking and taking in everything about a man, trying to put together who he truly was. Unfortunately, I was a sleuth with a glitch: I saw everything positive about a man and missed the big red signs of negative truth.

One time when I was at a guy's place I went to his kitchen to get some chips—and discovered three baby bottles. I asked this single guy, who had told me that he did not have any children, why he had baby bottles in his cabinet. He told me they were for his puppy. When I pointed out to him that he had no puppy, he told me that he was planning to surprise me with one for Christmas. I was so excited about getting the puppy that I forgot to ask him if the puppy was also going to be using the baby formula that I'd found. My glitch was hard at work on this particular day. Come Christmas I was gifted with his newborn daughter with her teen mom instead of the puppy I was expecting.

This experience led me to focus more on Truth V—getting the clues. If only I had asked more questions or been open to observing both the good and bad of the baby hider, I would have known early on that this was not the brother for me. But like a lot of you, I placed a lot of weight on what a brother said and paid little attention to what he actually did.

It is time to activate all of our senses and gain a better perspective on what our men are telling and showing us. Being a listener in full will lead you down the path toward a more fulfilling love life as you learn how to feed the great relationships and stop cold the negative ones. All it takes to be a listener in full is to be a keen and at times quiet observer.

❧ TRUTH V

GET THE CLUES

Being quiet gives you clues into what is truly going on in your relationship.

THE LOWDOWN

Being quiet at times is very hard for sisters to do. True silence is often viewed as being a waste of time or even distracting. Sisters, quiet is not distracting or a waste of time, but a proven way to connect to what is truly going on in any given situation. Have you ever had a disagreement with someone and been convinced of your point only to step away from the argument or sleep on it and then the next day totally get what the other person was saying? This is the power of quiet—to clue you in to what really is going on. Quiet offers sisters valuable insight.

Master this truth early. Truth V examines the power to gather and act on all of the clues that a man is giving you but not telling you directly. By getting the clues you will be able to determine early on in a relationship whether or not it is worth pursuing. By quietly monitoring his actions and listening to his conversation you will learn all you need to know within the first month of dating and not waste months or even years on bad relationships. My friend Georgia almost learned this truth too late in her relationship with Marco.

GEORGIA AND MARCO

Georgia is a 37-year-old single mother of two boys who is looking for a brother who is mature, loves kids, and is interested in being her partner for life. Two years ago Georgia met Marco at her older son's school fund-raiser. Marco was also a single father of two boys, one away at college and one a senior at the school that Georgia's son attended. After some lively conversation at the fund-raiser, Marco and Georgia continued their conversation later that evening over the phone.

After about four months of dating, Georgia thought it

was time to introduce Marco to her sons. When Marco came over for dinner Georgia noticed that he wasn't his usual outgoing self. Although he was friendly with the boys, it seemed as if Marco was a little put off by the occasion. Later that night after the boys had gone to bed Georgia called Marco to see how he was doing. Georgia quickly sensed by the tone of Marco's voice that he didn't want to talk all that much.

The following week Marco asked to meet Georgia for lunch, where he told her hesitantly that he wasn't sure that the relationship was working for him. He noted that they were both busy with their families and maybe that this was not the best time to get together. Georgia was caught off guard by the breakup. She had thought that she and Marco were slowly building toward something great and that they couldn't go wrong with their lives being so similar. Georgia was not sure what the problem was.

Weeks later we were discussing Marco over lunch and I asked Georgia if she thought that Marco's mood change might have had something to do with meeting her kids. She quickly said no because he was a family man himself with two boys. But when she thought back over their time together, she realized that while Marco had always seemed excited about his children and actively prepared each of them for future success, he spoke often about how much he was looking forward to his younger son going into college next year so that he could finally sell the large family house and move into a small houseboat on the lake. Marco was proud of his sons' achievements, but he was also looking forward to the fun, unrestricted life he would lead once his younger boy was away at school.

As we talked further about Georgia's conversations with Marco regarding kids it became clear to me that throughout their four months together Marco had shared numerous clues with Georgia that being a fill-in dad was not for him. Though he'd expressed excitement over having his daily parental responsibilities end, Georgia had taken these comments as meaning no *new* children. She'd never thought he meant he didn't want to help her raise her sons. It turned out that although Marco was extremely interested in Georgia, he had never had any interest in raising more children. Georgia had been too busy focusing on her relationship's potential and not listening to the brother's views of the next phase of his life.

A month later when I caught up with Georgia she told me that she and Marco had talked and that I was right about his concerns. He had been crazy about her and thought he could put his feelings about having more children to the side, but when he met the boys he saw that he couldn't be part of her life and not fall for her sons. Marco liked the boys, but he knew he would eventually come to regret the added responsibility. Although they are no longer seeing each other, Georgia and Marco remain good friends who bond over their mutual dedication to their children's success.

Marco and Georgia's situation mirrors many relationships. So many times we are clueless about the things that men are telling us early on that could circumvent problems down the road. In Georgia's case she had a man hinting around that he really was not interested in parenting again. If Georgia had focused a little more on Marco's responses and actions, she would have saved herself the frustration of trying to figure out why a great brother wanted out.

Getting the clues not only provides hints to negative underpinnings in a relationship, but can foreshadow positive events as well. Take the case of my girl Macy, who was able to buy the ideal gift for her man, Russell.

MACY AND RUSSELL

Russell was growing more and more frustrated with the fact that he could not get anywhere on time. Over the years he had invested in calendars, PDAs, special watches, and talking clocks. None of these items seemed to curtail his lateness.

One day while Russell was complaining yet again that he was late to a client meeting, Macy decided to do a little sleuthing of her own. She asked Russell what he was doing in the car that he couldn't seem to get anywhere on time. Russell told her that he was doing the usual things: listening to the radio or eating on the run. None of these things, he assured her, was slowing him down. The only time he slowed up during his day was when he took a call on his cell phone. It was just easier for him to hold on to the phone and concentrate on the caller if he pulled over on the side of the road. These calls were maybe a minute or less, so they weren't slowing him down either, he thought. Russell was still baffled as to why he just could not get anywhere on time.

Being the master sleuth, Macy knew exactly why Russell was always late. It was his cell phone after all. Russell sold copiers, and although his calls for service and sales orders were often short, he received close to fifty a day—the call volume was slowing Russell up. Macy knew exactly how to remedy the situation, and the next day she bought Russell a headset for his phone. The new headset allowed Russell to conduct business without slowing his travel time.

Observe what makes your man happy. Take the time to figure out what brings him joy, surprises him, or causes him to really loosen up and live in the moment. These are the things that you should provide him with more often so that he thinks that you are just the perfect mate. It is not that you are some "super sister"—it's just that you take the time to not only respond to his words, but also plug into his thoughts.

✤ TRUTHFUL LESSON

Don't be blind to subtleties. They can literally be lifesavers.

The next time you are talking with your man, plug into both his verbal and nonverbal dialog. Think about what you are hearing and question what you are not. Truth number five can be both a lifesaver and a time saver for the sister dealing with the very best black man.

✤ BARE NECESSITY

I WILL ACTIVELY LISTEN IN TOTAL TO THE WORLD AROUND ME.

TRUTH VI
BE THE PRIZE!

Braedon was the butt of many jokes for never

having a woman while in college. When we go around

his frat brothers today, I try to always look my best

and let my man have a little get-back.

—*Ariel, 32*

LaDawn,

I have been with my man for four years and it seems as if we are no longer connecting. There was a time in our relationship when I knew that I was all he wanted, but now I am beginning to question it because he just does not seem all that enthralled with me. I do everything for this man and I am constantly there for him for whatever he needs. I have been feeling lately that my presence just annoys him. He has even told me on several occasions that I need to stop running behind him and find a hobby, but I thought that men wanted a woman to take care of them. When I decided that he was the man for me I decided to turn into the caregiver that all men want. How is it that I want to take care of him and he just wants to flee?

Sister, you are driving this man crazy. He is sending you so many not-too-subtle signs that you need to get a life outside of him. When you guys first got together you probably had friends, hobbies, and interests that brought a fresh perspective to your conversations. Now all you have is him. The brother wants some room and he needs for you to have a diversion. You are giving him what you think he wants and are not really listening to what he is telling you. It is clear to me that the brother values you having a life instead of being his shadow 24/7. Stop giving the brother the version of you that you think he wants and give him the true you that he fell in love with.

seven

LET THE
ROOSTER CROW

*Y*ou know how when a guy does something so wonderfully sexy and great, you look to all other brothers to do the same thing? (It's not the healthiest of behaviors, but I slip into it myself from time to time. ☺) Well, I had one of these experiences with Boyfriend X. Boyfriend X is unforgettable because whenever we went out he would at some point during the evening lean over and say to me, "You know, you are the best-looking woman in here." Wow! Was this always true? No, of course not, but I will not deny its power to totally elevate my mood and make me feel special. I remember thinking at the time that someone had had to teach him to say this in order to impress women, but it happened all the time and it always came across as genuine. Why did he do this?

Years later when I reflect on this brother I now understand why he did it. The compliment was not totally about me. It was also about his need to feel superior to the other guys in the room. By saying that he was with the most beautiful woman in the room, he was able within his own mind to elevate his position in any social circle. Being with the hottest woman made him feel special. Me being impressed with his comment was just the icing on the cake.

❧ TRUTH VI

BE THE PRIZE!

Be the best for your man in every situation.

There is no better way to attract a great black man than to make him feel that you are simply the best woman out there for him. With your combination of charisma, intelligence, and hot looks, how in the world could he consider another woman? No matter where you go, you are the best thing in the room and absolutely no one can convince him differently. This is the truth that your mother never told you about. Always be your man's prize—the woman he always wanted but thought he never could get.

THE LOWDOWN

Men are natural competitors. They love to compare their jobs, cars, income, and homes all the time, every day of the week. Therefore it should come as no surprise to you that another area they like to compete in is the quality of woman they are able to attract. When I say quality of woman I am not referring to looks alone. Many men pride themselves on being with the most successful, intelligent, or charismatic woman, while other men like to be able to brag about a sister's ability to cook or sing. No matter what the bragging point is, men like to do it.

The key for sisters is to determine what it is that brings your man pride. Is it that his woman is the most physically attractive in the room? Then your goal should be to always be attractive for him so that you fulfill his need for superiority. Does he like to brag that you graduated at the top of your class? Then always be prepared to talk about how hard you worked in college and how challenging your latest project is. All of these actions will make your man feel that he is simply the luckiest brother in the room.

ARIEL AND BRAEDON

A good sister friend of mine, Ariel, believes strongly in this particular truth. Ariel knows that it is important that she always look her best for her fiancé, Braedon. The fact that she is the most attractive woman in the room goes a long way in making Braedon more aggressive and interactive in social situations. Having Ariel around makes Braedon feel great and adds to his self-confidence.

In the process of planning their wedding, Braedon has reached out to his old fraternity brothers to enlist their support as groomsmen. Planning the wedding has led

Braedon to revisit old feelings of inadequacy that he felt constantly when he was in college. While in college Braedon was the dorky guy who tutored the star athletes, making sure that they stayed eligible to play. In his sophomore year Braedon tried to change his image by pledging and then joining the fiercest fraternity on campus. But instead of improving his image he became the dork of the frat, known for never ever having a woman.

Almost ten years after graduating from college Braedon still at times feels insecure when he is around his fraternity brothers. No matter what level of success he has attained, Braedon knows that they only see him as the dorky mess that he was back in school.

The one thing that Braedon has over all of his other frat brothers is Ariel. Ariel is a 32-year-old customer service manager who moonlights as a bikini model. Braedon met Ariel when he had issues with getting new telephone service for his townhouse. He was surprised that after his problem was resolved she asked if she could call him. They laughed so hard that night on the phone, and they have been laughing and loving ever since.

Braedon cannot wait for his groomsmen to meet Ariel. Since they have been together Braedon rarely feels insecure. He finally has all the other guys beat.

Is all of this sounding a little too sexist to you? After all, isn't it demeaning for any woman to have to promote herself in order to aid a man's self-esteem? For once you may have to take the sexist edge off this particular approach and understand that because men are natural competitors they always want to feel that what they have is better than what the next man has. If you understand what he feels you have that no other woman has and heighten that quality, he will always see you as a prize that he is lucky to possess. This does not take anything away from the full picture of you, but what it does is allow you to feel the special glow of being simply the best woman for your man, and what woman doesn't want that?

Often sisters are caught off guard by what their men think is their hottest attribute. My girl Jillian was recently clued into what it is about her that her boyfriend Dion thinks is hot. Although she was flattered by the attention that Dion showed her, she never thought that he would be so impressed by her childhood obsession.

DION AND JILLIAN

Late one evening while Dion and Jillian were sipping some wine and listening to music, Jillian commented that when she was growing up she played the saxophone. Dion laughed. Jillian quickly corrected him and said that she hadn't just casually studied the sax—she'd been one of the best students in the area and really considered pursuing it as a career. Dion hadn't known that Jillian had a musical background—he'd been aware that she enjoyed going out with him to hear new bands, but he didn't know that she was able to really feel the music.

Weeks later when Jillian accompanied Dion to a club to assist one of the bands with setting up, he asked the sax man if his lady could give it a try. Dion explained that Jillian had played throughout school and he wanted to see if she was really as good as she had been bragging that she was. After a few minutes of hesitation Jillian placed the sax to her mouth and did much better than good—she was great. Dion was blown away that Jillian had this skill and had never even told him about it.

From that night on Dion always mentioned to his clients and friends that his lady was a musician. This made Jillian laugh because she had always considered herself an accountant, but the fact that she can play means a great deal to Dion, so she lets him gloat. His interest and excitement in her talent led her to take sax lessons again, so that she can recapture some of the magic from her youth.

But what if you are not sure what your man thinks is special about you? As I mentioned in chapter 6, you may at times have to play the detective when dealing with your man. The next time the two of you are out and he is introducing you to a new acquaintance, take note of his description of you and the ways that he includes you in the conversation. What topics does he always ask you about? What successes of yours does he tout? What was it that he was first attracted to? All of these questions are key indicators of what your man values in you.

After you investigate a bit, you can always ask him outright what he thinks sets you apart from the crowd. Take his answers and your investigative results and mix them with what you have known all your life about what makes you special. It is time to shine, sister, with full awareness that you are what your man wants and that you are truly as wonderful as you have always thought!

❧ TRUTHFUL LESSON

Always aim to be the star of the room in your man's eyes.

❧ BARE NECESSITY

I AM A UNIQUE CREATION WORTHY OF PRAISE.

TRUTH VII
BREAK THE
GIRLFRIEND CHAIN

I have been friends with Candy for twelve years

and there is always drama between her, her son's father,

and his new wife. When I met Bison and he told me

he had a six-year-old daughter, part of me couldn't

get up from the table fast enough.

—Trishelle, 31

LaDawn,

I have a girlfriend who is always talking bad about my man. Sometimes I think it's because she doesn't have one, but now some of the things she's said have made me start to question whether or not my man is really a good one. We have had our ups and downs, and my girl knows all about them and says I should get rid of him. However, I think this is normal and not an indicator that I should leave him. What do you think?

Don't ever judge your man based on what others say because you are the only person outside of your man who knows the real story on your relationship. What friends and family think should come second on your list when you are trying to decide if a brother is the one for you.

You have made the classic mistake that sisters make every day: seeking comfort in the conversation of your girlfriends and then being angry with them when they throw your relationship facts back at you weeks later. You gave your friend the info and now you are mad that she is still digesting it. That simply is not fair. If you want to keep your girl's opinions and judgments out of your relationship, then stop talking to her about it. Know that while you are able to forgive your man, she may not be able to. She is getting into your relationship only because you invited her in.

eight

⚛⚛⚛

DITCH THE SKIRT

_T_here is a sister I love dearly, but every time I talk to her she is on the lookout for relationship discord. It's as if she is always ready to jump in and knock a brother out. One time she called when I had a cold, and when I answered the phone with a scratchy voice she immediately asked, "You sound like you've been crying. Did he hit you?" Sister friend was getting her gloves on and coming over to watch my back. When I finally stopped laughing I had to really think if this was a good conversation to keep having.

This particular sister was having constant problems in her marriage. She and her husband had no problem getting physical. No matter how many times our circle rescued her from her abusive home, she would always find a reason to return to it. This sister lived in hell and pushed her hell onto others. After a few more raucous calls, I had to tell the sister that we would be better served by being just acquaintances. I just could no longer allow my relationship to be her focus.

Can't seem to get the quality brothers? Don't know why they will not approach you? The answer may be as simple as examining your sister circle. I know that I am going to get nailed for what I am about to say because Truth VII involves examining and perhaps changing what all sisters rely on to get through life—our sister circle.

Friendships keep us motivated and help feed our spirit. There is nothing like a sister circle to make you feel that you are not alone. Girlfriends can provide a source of comfort that our families and our men cannot always provide. But you know that for all the positive sisters in your circle, there is one who drains you—the sister who is always having drama in her relationships and looking to you to unload. There are some toxic girlfriends out there, and it is time to break these relationships off because often they are what is keeping you away from your very best black man.

❧ TRUTH VII

BREAK THE GIRLFRIEND CHAIN

Can't see any good men? Maybe your girl is standing in the way.

THE LOWDOWN

What we often don't realize is that in the same way you are what you eat, you also are what you choose to hang around. A girlfriend who is constantly complaining about her man, the lack of available black men, or how much she'd prefer to be on her own and doesn't need a man is subconsciously selling you on these ideals. Thinking in this fashion blinds you to the opportunities available to pursue great relationships with the best men.

There are some critical questions that you need to ask yourself when you are looking at your sister circle. Do any of your friends have the quality of man or relationship that you aspire to? Are you surrounding yourself with positive women who want what you want out of life? Do they date the kind of men that you find interesting? If the answer is no to these questions, then it is time to reconstruct your sister circle.

CANDY AND TRISHELLE

Trishelle almost lost her very best black man because of a toxic girlfriend. Trishelle and her friend Candy had been friends since they were teenagers. Candy was there for Trishelle through her college graduation and the process of buying her first house. Trishelle was there for Candy during her completion of basic training and the birth of her son Terrell. Their friendship in the beginning was one of mutual support where two good friends took the place of distant relatives and fair-weather acquaintances.

After Candy gave birth to Terrell her long-term boy-friend, Darnell, decided that he wanted Terrell in his life but not Candy. Darnell quickly arranged visitation and support for Terrell but made it clear to Candy that he was moving on in his romantic life. Candy dealt with this ar-rangement calmly for the most part because she knew that Darnell loved his son and was going to be active in his life. In Candy's mind Darnell would have to come back to her eventually in order to be the great dad he wanted to be.

She was greatly surprised that at Terrell's fourth-birthday party Darnell did not come alone. This time he brought his new fiancée with him. Candy seethed at the party, and as the wedding date approached she got more and more verbally abusive toward Darnell and vowed to make things involving Terrell as difficult as possible as pun-ishment for not choosing her.

Trishelle initially saw this period in Candy's life as being like all the other times when Candy would blow up and then the fire would slowly fizzle out, but this time the cool-ing out never happened. Candy is in a place that no amount of friendship consolation can heal. Trishelle has broken up enough fights between Candy and Darnell that at times Trishelle starts to think that Darnell is doing her wrong along with Candy. The truth is that Darnell moved on with his life and Candy is still stuck on what could have been.

All of these activities have led Trishelle to establish a no-child rule when it comes to brothers. No matter how mature a brother is, she stays away if he has children. Trishelle figures that she gets enough baby daddy stress from Candy every night on the phone and doesn't need to bring it to her own table.

One night Trishelle and Candy decided to go out to a local hotel bar to listen to jazz and grab some drinks. While sitting at the bar Trishelle noticed a fine brother playing the cello. He had butterscotch-colored skin and long brown dreads that appeared to move in rhythm with his fingers. The small professor glasses that he wore only added to the mad-artist vibe that Trishelle so loved in her men. After he finished his session, Bison introduced himself to both Candy and Trishelle and then proceeded to spend the rest of the evening getting to know Trishelle better. In the process of giving the usual stats Bison said that he was the father of a 6-year-old girl. Trishelle's mood instantly wilted. Bison appeared to be a great guy: talented, interesting, and attentive. Now she'd have to throw him back because he had baggage.

While Trishelle soaked up information from Bison she felt Candy kicking her under the bar, giving her the universal sign to cut it off. When he excused himself to go back and play, five seconds did not pass before Candy started her "They are all the same" routine. Trishelle knew all too well that kids add drama to relationships, but this time she was curious enough to test the waters. When Candy picked up her purse from the bar to leave, Trishelle decided to stay until the next break. She knew Candy was mad at her for not leaving with her, but Bison was the most interesting prospect that Trishelle had met in months. She decided that it was time for her to start living her life instead of continually running scared from Candy's.

Our girlfriends mean the world to us, but often they are the one thing standing between us and the incredible love that we so desire. In this case it was apparent to Trishelle that Candy's negative experiences had begun to shape Trishelle's own choices in men. She consciously chose men at the opposite spectrum of Candy's experience. Not all sisters have this clarity when it comes to how much of an influence their friends have over their personal lives. Sometimes our friends are holding us captive and we don't even know it.

LILLY

Lilly is a 31-year-old newlywed who was basking in the excitement of her new marriage and all the trappings of setting up a home with her husband, Dexter. Lilly is a reporter for the local paper and during the last four years has struck gold as a part-time freelancer focusing on stories on inner-city children. As a result of her double duty, Lilly is financially very comfortable. Two years ago she bought her first house, which she and Dexter now share. Dexter is an art teacher during the day and a struggling sculptor at night. His goal is to put together enough great pieces by the end of the year to hold a show and eventually step away from teaching. Lilly has always been supportive of Dexter's dream but has been wondering lately if she has set herself up to be taken advantage of.

Although Dexter and Lilly are extremely happy together, Lilly was concerned about the division of the expenses in the house. Did Dexter expect her to continue to fund the restoration of the house on her own? Was he interested in splitting things 50–50 or was he going to jump into the role of managing the finances, which would result in Lilly losing control over her savings and earnings? Lilly was starting to get concerned because it appeared that Dexter was never interested in sitting down and hammering out their financial future. Was Dexter going to carry his fair share or bottom out and feed off her like so many other men had tried to?

After a few weeks of evading the subject Lilly finally sat Dexter down to discuss their financial obligations. Lilly made it clear to Dexter that he would have to carry his weight and that she would not be working herself to death to take care of them forever.

Dexter was caught off guard by the strength of Lilly's comments. He had always carried his weight in the relationship and had been quiet on the subject recently only because he wanted to focus on pulling all of his financial information together before sitting down and making decisions. Dexter was a little offended that Lilly would even think that he would simply spend all her money. He knew how hard she worked and he would never disrespect her like that.

In the end Lilly had to apologize for attacking Dexter. He was right that he had always carried his own weight, and she knew that he would never just drop his job to pursue his dream. Lilly explained to Dexter that she had known too many men who had worked their women to death only to discard them when there was nothing else left. When Dexter asked who had done this to her, however, Lilly could not think of one person. She then realized that the basis of her fear of being taken advantage of rested with her friend Sulie and not with anything that had ever happened directly to her.

Sulie and Lilly had been friends since college, and soon after college Sulie married one of their fellow classmates, Charles, who was on his way to medical school. While Charles was in medical school and completing his residency Sulie worked hard as a schoolteacher and moonlighted as a tutor to take care of them both.

Sulie rarely had time to get together, and when Lilly did see her, Sulie always looked tired. Although Sulie never complained about her situation, Lilly saw the wear and tear. Sulie was putting in the long hours with no immediate reward. The only thing that she held on to was that in two years when Charles finished his residency she could take some time off and maybe have a few kids or go back to school. She was looking forward to settling down into a normal life.

Sulie got her break in two years, but not the one that she planned. Once he completed his residency, Charles decided that he wasn't really ready for a "normal life." Charles and Sulie are in the midst of a long divorce where all she really wants is a small settlement in return for all the support she gave Charles. She bought into his dream and was left quietly holding the bag.

Although Sulie never talked in great detail about Charles and how she felt about taking care of him all those years, Lilly silently observed her friend's situation. Somewhere along the way Lilly had built an argument against taking care of any man when no man had actually ever asked her to.

Lilly made the mistake of internalizing a sister friend's situation and bringing it into her current relationship. Even though on a conscious level she knew that Dexter was always going to carry his weight, Lilly felt the need to make sure he was clear on a point that had absolutely nothing to do with their relationship. Allowing your girlfriends' relationship situations to shape the concerns of *your* relationship will lead to a lot of pointless arguments and needless boundaries.

❦ TRUTHFUL LESSON

Remove negative influences that shortchange your happiness.

In dealing with the very best black man, everything about you has to be on point—including your friends. You do not know how many men I hear from who say that their girlfriend's friends have had a disabling effect on their relationship. Toxic girlfriends give bad advice, make you question your relationship decisions, and cannot share in the joy of a positive relationship. It is time to break the toxic girlfriend chain.

❦ BARE NECESSITY

I WILL REMOVE FROM MY LIFE PEOPLE WHO DRAIN ME.

TRUTH VIII
LIVE FOR YOU

If a woman allows a man to walk all over her

or be continuously unreliable, he is never going

to take her seriously. If she doesn't value her time

and attention, why should I?

—*Felix, 36*

LaDawn,

I have been dating this guy for two years and he really wants to get married. The problem is that after a long break I have decided to go back to school at night and when I talk to him about it he doesn't seem real excited about it. I know that he expects me to be at home for meals, conversation, and all of the special times that couples share, but how can I not pursue my education?

Love can be a tricky balancing game when you are trying to keep yourself happy and still meet the needs of your partner. In every relationship there has to be a "me" line—you are willing to do whatever it takes to keep your relationship going as long as it doesn't stop your personal growth.

Your man should not be selfish. In this case you have to go with what will best benefit your development. Even the best relationships sometimes end, and you would truly regret not getting the education thing done when you could. The brother is going to have to understand that your personal development is just as important as his relationship needs. He should want you to be the very best that you can be.

nine

⚜

I LOVE ME

*P*ersonally, I do not believe in rules. Rules have that whole right-and-wrong thing attached that I have never bought into. But there is one rule that has slipped into my overall approach to life that I cannot let go of: always do for you first. This may sound incredibly pompous and selfish, but truly it is the only way to guarantee the following:

- ❧ That your needs are met
- ❧ That others get the best from you
- ❧ That you can happily meet others' needs

Crazy-sounding but true. It is only through being good to yourself that you can freely give to others with no regrets.

All of us have been around generous sisters who are drained and underappreciated. They are waiting for someone to be as good to them as they have been to others. Sadly, this reciprocation rarely happens. By giving so much to others and not getting anything in return, all a sister is left with is a future filled with few opportunities for happiness. It is time to act on Truth VIII—live for you!

Before Truth VIII entered my life, I had been pretty secure with my ability to attend to my needs over those of a brother, especially when it involved tremendous sacrifice for me and little sacrifice for him. But like most things in life, there is always a test case—that one brother who is able to slide past the radar and take a little too much, with or without you knowing it. Here starts the tale of Coat Brother.

I was crazy about Coat Brother. There was nothing that he could do that I wouldn't go along with because he was romantic, giving, and, well, a hottie. You know, hot brothers sometimes slide past the radar a lot easier. Coat Brother, for all of his good points, had one critical flaw—he could not keep a job. Every three months or so I would receive a call that Coat Brother needed me to come and pick him up from his latest failed job. Money was always tight for him, and prior to learning Truth VIII I was willing to support him in any way that I could if it meant he would eventually get himself together.

One day Coat Brother came to me and asked if I would help him get some new clothes and a coat for his next great job adventure. This was going to be a more corporate environment, and he assured me that he would pay me back. I knew on some level that this was not going to work out in my favor, but off we went to the mall, Coat Brother and Sucker Sister, to outfit him for his new job. My reasoning was that maybe my helping him would give him more of an incentive to help himself.

A few days later I stopped by Coat Brother's place to surprise him with dinner and noticed that his car was not in the parking lot. Apparently he had not arrived home from work, so I decided to wait a few extra minutes for him. Five minutes later his car pulled up and he hopped out, but he was not alone—there was a woman with him. Initially I decided to sit back and see what exactly was going on. I never wanted to be the kind of sister who just goes off on a brother when he is with another woman and she turns out to be a cousin or something—that's never cool.

As he and the sister got out of the car they wrapped their arms around each other and he bent down to kiss her. Obviously this was not a relative. Super Sister popped into action, and I sprang out of the car. Not only did he stand there looking stupid in the coat that I had just bought him, but when she turned to talk to me I saw that *she* was wearing one of the sweaters that I had bought him.

The end of this story is ugly—it involved a lot of running around and cussing in a parking lot and ended with his coat landing somewhere in the middle of an intersection—but this truly is not the point. The point is that I knew when I went shopping with him that this was too much for me to do and that he was definitely the wrong person to do it for. I was not thinking about what I needed and what I was truly willing to do. I was trying to be the miracle worker—the one who would turn his life around. In the end I got played.

You are important! Sisters, it is time to drop the baggage of doing for others and neglecting ourselves. The truth is that no matter how much you do for others they will never be totally satisfied, and in the process you have lost valuable time when you could have been proactively working to improve your life.

Often when we meet someone we consider an ideal man we begin to live for this man and focus on fulfilling his every need. There is nothing wrong with satisfying another unless it always comes at your own expense. For example, how many times have you changed your schedule to meet his schedule, neglected your studies or work to lie in bed an extra hour with him, or given up valued friendships and activities because your lover doesn't approve? These changes are okay in small doses, especially when you know that your man is doing some adjusting too, but if you are always the one inconvenienced, then you are not getting what you deserve.

❧ TRUTH VIII

LIVE FOR YOU!

Treat yourself well and others will follow your lead.

THE LOWDOWN

In order to be confident, well rounded, and interesting, you have to feed your spirit. Feeding your spirit means doing the things that bring you joy and keep your brain energized. Every day there should be activities and interests that you pursue that serve the sole purpose of placing you on a higher plane.

Fulfilling your own needs is important because it is the only way to make sure that the very best man knows that you can handle yourself with or without him. It is crucial that any prospective suitor knows that you are happy to be with him, but if he were not in your life you would be okay as well. This lesson is important in that the very best black man does not want a woman who will be totally dependent on him for meeting all of her financial, emotional, and social needs. He wants a sister to be able to carry her own weight.

BRIE AND FELIX

This truth was recently reinforced by my friend Brie's boyfriend, Felix, who told me that one of the main reasons he was drawn to Brie was that she never waited for him to do anything. If Brie wanted to go to a play, she purchased the tickets and then asked him if he wanted to go. If Felix wasn't interested in Brie's latest adventure, then she'd come up with a friend who wanted to go or simply go by herself. When she wanted to paint her bedroom, Brie did not wait for Felix to do it. She went ahead and did it herself. Felix is a professional painter and probably would have done a better job, but Brie did it herself because in her mind she'd painted every other room in her house, so why stop now? After she'd finished Felix came in and offered to paint the floorboards. The room was perfect.

In Felix's view Brie's independence is hot because he knows that no matter what happens to him she will always be able to handle things. Brie is with Felix because she loves him and not because he is so handy around the house. Felix has never, ever been attracted to clingy women.

Now, note that most men will balk and bristle on the surface when it comes to a woman who is unwilling to change her schedule or has an interest that he does not understand, but ladies, know that this frustration does not last for long and he will eventually get over it. The bristling is about control. As much as men think that they want to run a woman, most were raised by independent women and would run away screaming from any woman who is constantly looking to him to make decisions and orchestrate her life. The secret to maintaining power in a relationship is realizing that you bring as much to the table as he does and that your thoughts, hobbies, and interests are just as important.

Be an active participant in your relationship. Have opinions and ideas that will increase the level of relationship success. There is no faster way to lose ground in a relationship than never to have anything to say about its growth. If one partner is always the most vocal regarding relationship decisions, you will find that partner is the one who is both the most fulfilled and the most burdened in the relationship. His burden is that he wants to please you but has no idea what you need and want. The decision maker is fulfilled in the sense that he gets to make the major decisions in the relationship, but he is also burdened because the decisions he makes may run contrary to your plans and you won't tell him what you want.

It is paramount that you maintain a sense of control in your romantic life. The easiest way to do this is to speak up regarding the things that you need in life and from the relationship. I promise you that if you step up to the plate in this regard you will find that you are much happier and more fulfilled in your relationship.

While you should live for yourself, there are some sisters who take this truth a little too far. Here are three actions that the very best black man is not going to go for:

❦ Telling him that you are seeing other men
❦ Confronting him loudly in public
❦ Flirting with other men when he is there

Sometimes sisters who are truly brazen try to pass off these moves as things that they just have to do, and if he can't deal with it, he has to go. Sisters, if you take any of the actions listed above, the very best man is going to leave. If he doesn't bristle at these three actions, then there is something wrong with this brother and *you* need to leave. Living for you enhances your relationship experience. In no way should it jeopardize that experience.

❦ TRUTHFUL LESSON

The key to ultimate happiness is you.

Pursue those positive things that are critical to you being who you need to be in order to be fulfilled. The very best black man will be drawn to your sense of purpose and to the fact that you want the very best for yourself and can be an equal partner in the relationship's success.

❧ BARE NECESSITY

THE POWER TO BE HAPPY COMES FROM ME.

TRUTH IX
FRIENDSHIP
TRULY MATTERS

Only a man who is your friend can look at you

at your physical worst and say that you are still

the most beautiful woman that he has ever met.

—Monica, 26

LaDawn,

I have a great male friend that I am thinking should be more than that. Should I ruin a great friendship hoping for more?

Friendships are often a great first step toward a lasting love. I would encourage you to move forward with the love thing if your guy friend has indicated that he would like to be more to you as well. Contrary to the myth that is out on the streets, when a relationship between a man and a woman who were friends first doesn't work out, it is possible to make a transition back to the just-friends thing. So you may not have anything to lose by simply trying it out. In my opinion friends often make the best lovers because you have something concrete to hold on to when relationship bumps pop up.

ten

A FRIEND
WITH BENEFITS

*L*ike the one you are with! This truth is huge when it comes to developing long-term relationships. Simple as it seems, often we fall for men that we really do not like. You know what I am talking about: the brother has the hard body and the swagger, but you can't stand the way he talks. Or the career-minded brother who seems to always focus on what you are doing wrong. These are the men that you are drawn to, even fall in love with, but if you were truly honest with yourself, you would acknowledge that you don't really like them all that much.

I remember a time when I was dating a brother that my family and friends thought was wonderful. He was an educated, successful, and caring brother—the perfect boyfriend who appeared to be the one. Slowly over the year or so that we dated he was winning over everyone in my life . . . except for me.

Perfect Boyfriend had me perplexed because I saw all the good things that everyone else around me saw, but I still could not take him seriously. What was it that was turning me off? What made me not buy into the fact that this relationship was it?

One day I realized exactly what the problem was. Perfect Boyfriend was wonderful at attaching himself to my circle, but he sucked at attaching himself to me. On numerous occasions we would be out with his friends or coworkers and he would literally leave me by myself to go off to talk to someone else. At other times he would strike up conversations with strangers without even the slightest acknowledgment that I was standing right there. These scenarios occurred all the time.

The final straw came for me when we went shopping together out of state and he began a conversation with the salesgirl while I browsed. When I came to him to ask his opinion on a shoe he shushed me and asked me if I saw that he was talking. The first thing that came to my mind was to clobber him right in front of the dim-witted salesgirl. Not wanting to spend the night in lockup, I quietly left the store and let him continue his conversation. I got into my car, in which we both had driven there, and left Perfect Boyfriend to hoof it back two hours into the city.

Truth IX serves as an answer to my situation and many other perplexing relationship dramas. Make sure that the man you are with is your friend. If he isn't deeply connected to you or doesn't share interests with you outside of just your body, then he is not the very best black man for you. In every relationship there comes a time when you will need more of a friend and supporter than a lover. It is during these times that you will be thankful for your man's laughter, quick wit, and sense of decorum.

Other times the fact that you really just like your man will be the only thing keeping you in the relationship. How many times have you had a disagreement and then your man said something silly and you both cracked up laughing and momentarily you forgot what you were fighting about? Sometimes all you have to hold on to is a great friend. Liking your man and considering him a friend will always get you over relationship hurdles.

❧ TRUTH IX

FRIENDSHIP TRULY MATTERS

Truly liking your man adds foundation to your relationship. In downtimes liking him is all that you have.

THE LOWDOWN

Only get involved with a brother who would make a great friend. If you meet a man and you know without a doubt that if you were a classmate or a colleague of his that you would value his thoughts, find him funny, or think he would provide you with great advice, then this is a great man to pursue. A man who is your friend is more likely to be interested in who you are on the inside and will be a great co-pilot as you head through the many stages of life.

The truth is that when relationships get strained there are only two things that keep you in the room: the brother is hot as hell, and regardless of whatever it is that you are fighting about he is still your favorite person in the world.

When I say best friend I know a lot of you are shaking your head and saying that a man can never be better than your best girlfriend. Well, here is a flash, sisters—the very best black man expects to be your partner in the relationship. Partnership means equal time and attention when it comes to everything that concerns you. Partners expect to be part of every decision, triumph, and heartache. This man will know things about you that your girlfriends will never know, and you will share experiences with him that your girlfriends will never get to share. He is the best friend possible—a friend with benefits.

MONICA AND CHRIS

My girlfriend Monica learned this valuable truth when she was dating Chris. Chris was a wonderful brother who Monica knew had the potential to be great husband material, a hard worker who still took the time to cater to her every need. About six months into their relationship Monica discovered a lump in her breast. She was only 26 years old. After numerous doctors' appointments it was determined that she had breast cancer that would be best treated with a mastectomy and chemotherapy.

When Monica told Chris about her diagnosis she was scared that he wouldn't be interested in sticking around during her treatment and recovery. A lot of the things that they loved doing together would have to be placed on the back burner while she underwent treatment. Adding to Monica's stress were the physical changes that she was going through and whether or not Chris would still find her sexy. Chris often bragged about Monica's long jet-black hair and her hourglass shape, and these things plus other aspects of her physical self were going to change as the result of treatment. Although they had not talked about having children, she had watched Chris with his nephews on many Saturday afternoons and noticed his sheer joy in their presence. This was a man who loved kids, and now she might not be able to give them to him. Monica thought for sure that Chris would decide that this was too much to take on.

However, Monica was surprised to find out that Chris understood what she was fighting. Daily he sent her e-mails with news stories on how others had beat cancer. When her hair started to fall out he bought them matching caps with the logo of their favorite sports team so that she would not feel alone when they went out. When Monica mentioned that she felt bad about not being physically up for their marathon lovemaking sessions, Chris sent her a giant card that said, "I have waited 33 years for the best sex of my life. A few months' wait to get it back is nothing." Monica was fortunate to have chosen as her mate a man who was her friend as well as her lover. Chris made what was an extremely challenging experience easier by simply being supportive.

Get a brother who can be your friend. When you are friends you develop a secret language and way of communicating that others will never be able to crack. You know that relationship will endure the ups and downs of time because there is more keeping you together than just the superficial. In the end your relationship is more successful because you have much more to lose than just a boyfriend or husband—you could also possibly lose your best friend for life.

❀ TRUTHFUL LESSON

Sometimes all you have to hold on to is your best friend. Make sure that he is able to be yours.

A man who is your friend is able to be supportive, loving, and insightful. He has the ability to make you laugh and love yourself at the same time. You develop a personal language and inside jokes. When your lover is your friend you never ever lose that across-the-room aspect of your relationship: the feeling that only the two of you get each other and everything and everyone else in the room is secondary.

❀ BARE NECESSITY

I WILL ONLY BE INVOLVED WITH THOSE WHOM I GENUINELY LIKE.

TRUTH X
ALWAYS REMEMBER
THE FIRST TIME

When I first met Malik I was just blown away

by the intensity of his eyes. Each time he looked

at me I felt he was peering deep into my soul.

—Dana, 29

LaDawn,

My husband has turned into a couch potato and he is not the sexy man that I married five years ago. His wardrobe consists of sweats and T-shirts and the only time I see a suit is on the major holidays. Where did my sexy brother go? How can I let him know that I love him, but I really miss the old him?

Brothers complain all the time that sisters change in relationships but totally miss that they get comfortable and complacent as well in relationships. Your man just needs a refresher course on what made him desirable when you guys first met. Maybe you should break out the old photo album or your wedding photo or have a discussion about what you found so appealing when you were first dating. Sometimes you have to bring things back to the forefront so that he can clearly see how sexy he once was.

You may even want to take him shopping for a new sexy look or have a couple's spa day with massage and beauty treatments to trigger his inner hotness. The key is to get him back to the days when you first met and those things that made you hot for each other.

eleven

THE HOTNESS

*W*henever there arises a time when I can't exactly remember what it was about my husband that pulled me in, I only have to think of one night—our night at the jazz club. It was raining that night, and we went to a local jazz club to grab dinner and listen to the band. JB showed up in the sexiest shirt and jeans with a long trench coat that I thought was just too cute, but the thing that sealed the deal for me was that he was wearing cowboy boots. I had never seen a brother wear cowboy boots before, and I thought that this was a brother who was both confident and comfortable. I *had* to get a little bit of this.

That evening I was swept away by how he handled himself. JB possessed a command of the room that I had never witnessed before, and everyone was pulled in by his charm and wit. I was special because he was special. And I never felt that he wanted to be anywhere else but with me at that small club that night. Even today I still get giddy thinking about this evening. So the next time I walk into our family room and JB is camped out on the couch watching yet another episode of sports something-or-other with our son passed out next to him, I only have to go back to that day at the club to realize that my exciting and sexy man hasn't exactly gone away—he's only taking a brief time-out to hang with his little partner in crime.

There is something to be said for the first time you meet someone and that spark of interest is ignited. Right at this exact moment there is no one else in the world even close to being more interesting. During this very special moment all you see is greatness and opportunity. There is little room for quirks or negative traits. You are entering the honeymoon stage of a relationship, when adventure is always around the corner. Right at this exact moment you are in the eye of perfection, and all you want to do is stay there forever.

Inevitably the spark starts to fade and the petty quirks and real-life situations start to creep in. Day-to-day struggles and the normalcy of knowing each other too well kick in. At times you look over to former Mr. Hotness and struggle to remember what exactly it was about him that you just could not tear yourself away from. You begin to question your judgment. Was he ever hot, interesting, smart, or responsible? Could the sex have been mind-blowing and you just forgot? When exactly did the silk robe turn into old sweatpants and the same old T-shirt every night? Welcome to the world of an established relationship!

✿ TRUTH X

ALWAYS REMEMBER THE FIRST TIME

Remember often what it was that attracted you to your man and he to you.

When these moments arise in your relationship with your very best black man, it is important to reconnect to what it was that initially attracted you. Think back to your first sighting and what it was about him that you just could not ignore. Reconnecting in this way will allow you to recharge the passion and see that although you both are now much more comfortable with each other, none of the fundamentals of why you are with him has changed.

MALIK AND DANA

Truth X plays an important role in the relationship of my friends Malik and Dana. They have been living together for three years and are well down the road of relationship domesticity. Although each of them is still very attracted to the other, there are times in their relationship when one or the other is thinking, "Is this all there is?"

A huge issue in their relationship is Malik's constant criticism of Dana's laid-back way of approaching life. In

Malik's eyes, Dana at 29 has not decided who she is or what she wants to be. As they look at marriage in another year or so, he is scared that Dana will still be fluttering about between careers and interests and he will be left holding the provider bag. Not that Malik minds being the provider, but he can't even rely on the fact that Dana would allow him to make the financial decisions. He knows that she will still do whatever she wants no matter who is paying the bills.

Dana, on the other hand, recently shared with me her feeling that Malik doesn't like her very much anymore. He constantly harps on her latest hobbies and criticizes her for not taking her work more seriously. She is perplexed by Malik's actions because he knows that she just hasn't found the career/interest balance that she is looking for. Until she gets her dream job, she plans on continuing to sample the field. She has always earned a good living and has never been fired from any job. When she first met Malik he encouraged her to continue pursuing her dreams. Now he has grown increasingly more controlling in their relationship. Dana use to find his directness stabilizing; now it seems to only drive her up the wall.

Dana and Malik need to reflect on Truth X. In the beginning Dana was drawn to Malik's ability to handle any situation and get things done. When they first met Malik was opening his second Internet café and working on plans for a third. Malik was a brother who stuck to his dreams and made them happen. Dana hoped he would work the same magic for her.

When Malik first met Dana she came into one of his cafés offering to jazz it up with a mural at no charge in exchange for publicity for her design company. Not only was he impressed with her sketchbook, but also he was impressed with her worldview. Dana wasn't cynical or money-hungry like a lot of sisters Malik had come across. Her eye for color and detail had been an incredible asset to the second café. She did more than just the mural—she jumped right in and did the tabletops too, because she thought the room needed more color. Dana enjoyed doing her own thing, and all she ever expected from Malik was that he not get in her way.

Now here they were, both hating the very characteristics that initially brought them together. My answer to both Dana and Malik was to journey back to the time when they first met and were drawn to each other. Malik was just about to open his second café and was on his knees with the rest of his crew installing the tile flooring when in walked Dana. Malik hoped that she was responding to the Help Wanted sign out front and not just one of the lost tourists he got all day. Dana wasn't lost, and Malik quickly was pulled into her web of possibility and light.

Dana remembered seeing Malik working with the guys when she walked in, and when he identified himself as the owner she hoped that he wasn't as uptight as his khakis and polo shirt hinted. As it turned out, Malik wasn't uptight—he was really a cool guy, and Dana was impressed that he was able to accomplish so much at such a young age. Maybe she could pick up some business advice from him while she worked on the mural.

By just taking a minute to relive the moment they first met, they both realized that in many ways they still feel the same about each other. Instead of focusing on the daily differences, Malik and Dana chose to go back to a time when those differences were viewed as relationship strengths, not detractors. Although there are still times when the differences pop up, Dana and Malik are able to better appreciate them as the instigators of their relationship and not reasons for division.

Another important part of remembering the first time is reconnecting to that initial spark of attraction. Remember when he had the hottest body that you'd ever seen? Does he even recall how crazy he was about you in your short skirts? Once we have been in a relationship for a while, we all have a tendency to stop doing the special things that made us attractive to our partners. Most of the reason that the magic is gone from our relationships is because somewhere along the way we have forgotten to be appealing.

Reach back into that old arsenal of tricks for those devilish dresses and towering heels. Tell your man that you would love to see him get dressed up for dinner or grow back that goatee. Make a date and instead of getting dressed together like you normally do, dress at work or at a hotel and meet your man at your favorite spot. You will be amazed at how just walking through a strange door dressed super-hot and playing the pickup game with each other can really rekindle that old heat.

❧ TRUTHFUL LESSON

Always remember the first time you met. Every day seek out that special moment.

Breathe new life into your relationship! Reflect with your man on what it was that brought you two together. Having this moment will place everyday activities into context and provide you with a refresher on why your man is still the best brother for you!

❦ BARE NECESSITY

I WILL USE MY BEGINNINGS AS FUEL FOR MY FUTURE.

TRUTH XI
GET YOUR
DATING MIX ON

The dating world has changed so much.

I am hooked on sexy e-mails and camera phones

as seduction tools.

—*Lori, 36*

LaDawn,

I am a sister who is addicted to dating older men. I am 30 years old and I like to date men in their 40s and 50s for their financial stability and intellect. The downside is that older men often have adult children, ex-wives, and pasts that are so thick that a sister can get suffocated under all of the baggage. I am starting to reconsider what I am looking for in a man and am considering dating men my age, but honestly, where in the world would I start to find a brother my age who is just as intelligent, financially stable, and smooth as my cherished older brothers?

You need to stop chasing the older brothers because you have made it so clear that you have found their lives to be a lot more than what you are willing to deal with at this point in your life. The way to find the exact characteristics that you are looking for in a brother your own age is to use one of the new online dating methods or an executive dating service. Both of these options utilize the latest technology and screening methods to get you hooked up with brothers who have the unique qualities that you are looking for.

You are a sister looking for a special man who won't be found in just any club or on a street corner. Shake up your dating methods to make sure you get the brother of your dreams.

twelve

COMPUTER LOVE

$\mathcal{I}$ have been that sister who looks up after a healthy season of dating only to see that bars, clubs, churches, and gas stations as pickup points have burned me out. (Yeah, I said gas stations—don't knock it till you try it!) We have all had that moment when what we really want to know is, is this all there is when it comes to dating? Are we destined to blow our vocal cords yelling our names over manufactured beats? Do we have to have dinner with every single man who works with our sister? Do we have to give every man we meet the chance to disappoint us just because this one might be different? Dating is a lot of work.

I knew that traditional dating had grown dull for me when I realized that dinner and a movie was more about getting to see the new releases than it was about getting to know the great new guy. I had been to all of the hot restaurants, and if one more brother stepped up to me with the idea of going horseback riding or whitewater rafting, I really thought that I would just give up on dating altogether. I was comatose for a few months, pondering where in the world I could meet a fresh crop of guys and not waste my time playing the get-to-know-you game with guys that in the end I did not want to get to know.

My saving grace in the dating scene was the creation of singles nights at the local art gallery. In Washington, D.C., there is so much to do and many brothers to meet, but where were the brothers who loved the arts and music? I decided to place myself where the art lovers were. I signed up for special singles memberships at local galleries, theaters, and museums. Through these events I was able to meet brothers who had the same interests I did while supporting the creative works that I love. These events were perfect for me because they were no-pressure dating scenes that provided an easy screening process. Plus if a particular event did not yield a potential great man, I could still enjoy an exhibit, play, or benefit. I finally decided to date outside of the box. I got into the mix.

Better batches of brothers are out there for the taking. What you need to do is strategically place yourself where these brothers are. News flash, sisters: *great men are not in the clubs!* This is one of those things Mom told you that actually is dead-on. The truth is that there may be good brothers in the clubs, but the club environment just does not lend itself to interesting conversation, insight, or one-on-

one attention—which basically kills any chance at getting a good read on a new brother. Also, take this bit of advice: any guy your single friends hook you up with who is "just great for you" usually isn't. If the brother was so great, your girl would be with him. She isn't—and there is a reason why.

❧ TRUTH XI

> **GET INTO THE MIX**
>
> Looking for an exceptional relationship? Do exceptional things to get it.

THE LOWDOWN

Dating has so many facets. I am constantly amazed that sisters are so hesitant to try new ways to meet men. With the growth of online matches, the personals, dating services, and speed dating, no sister should be sitting at home on a Saturday night.

The truth is that these nontraditional ways of dating have worked for many people because they offer something that traditional dating has slowly moved away from— the opportunity to get to know someone before really physically connecting with him. With online dating and the personals you have to talk, entice, and entertain. There is that old-fashioned brain play that is circumvented when physical play is introduced first.

Sisters, what do you have to lose? Mix up your dating repertoire. Look into these new and exciting ways to date:

Speed Dating

Speed dating consists of five- to eight-minute rounds of dating with up to twenty-five guys a night.

Pros: This is one of the quickest ways to meet brothers who have signed up to meet you. No need to waste hours with the wrong guy—only minutes. It's a great way to date and even have fun with your girls—speed dating almost feels like you are part of a huge love-themed game show.

Cons: The great guys get moved around the room fast, and after sitting with twenty-five other ladies they may decide that you are not the best catch of the night. Some sisters are uncomfortable with the competition that goes into impressing someone within a short time frame. He may not send you that coveted follow-up e-mail that says that there was a connection, and there is little that you can do about it because no phone numbers can be exchanged the night of the speed-dating event.

Online Dating Services

The personal ad has grown up. Don't limit yourself to five lines in the personals section of your local paper. Get your own page and photo on some of the hottest relationship sites on the Web.

Pros: On the Web you get more room to describe yourself and what you are looking for. You can post fun photos and search other bios and photos for your ideal match. Your search now can go worldwide—allowing for more opportunities to meet unique brothers who have just what you are looking for.

Cons: There are so many people with pages on these sites that at times it can get overwhelming. Also, some brothers just never give up and keep sending you e-mail when you're not interested.

Lock and Key Parties

The sixties swinger game is back. You buy a lock, a brother buys a key, and you circulate for two hours looking for your match. In the sixties your match had to bed you—today he only has a great excuse to get to know you better.

Pros: Here's a low-cost dating option that guarantees that you will meet and have something to talk about with every guest at a party. Also, it's another great dating event for you and your girls. The pool of men is varied and wide. Never thought about dating a younger brother? Well, here is your chance!

Cons: The fact that it is low-cost means that any brother with $5 is probably in the room. There really isn't a screening process involved, so you are going to meet a lot of men who hold no interest for you.

Upscale Singles Nights

Sign up for a membership at museums, libraries, galleries, theaters, and much more. They often sponsor singles nights or other activities.

Pros: This is a great screening tool for finding brothers with similar interests. Events throughout the year allow for many chance meetings with a guy you have your eye on. If the dating thing isn't working out, you can always sit back and enjoy the event.

Cons: Some of the memberships can be pretty high-cost. Make sure that you are interested in the event or cause as well as the potential dating pool.

These methods have a built-in bonus for success because anyone you meet through these channels has paid for the privilege to meet someone great. They are less likely to waste their time, money, and energy just collecting numbers for no reason other than to fatten up their two-way.

LORI

I had a listener by the name of Lori who reached out to me. She was newly divorced with custody of her two teenage daughters. Lori counted herself as lucky in that she was making the single-mom thing work and her ex-husband remained an active dad and a pretty good friend. As the months after the divorce moved on, Lori decided to slowly rejoin the ranks of daters. It had been more than fifteen years since Lori had dated, so she had to learn quickly what was acceptable and unacceptable dating behavior.

Jumping back into the dating scene was daunting because Lori was getting into areas that she had never even considered in her twenties. There were younger men, men with children, co-workers, good-time men, and much more that Lori was not really sure what to do with. She realized quickly what she did not want in a brother, but it seemed that she would have to date every brother before getting to those few who were a good fit.

After months of doing the dinner-and-a-movie thing, the dinner-at-a-friend's-house thing, or the let's-meet-for-drinks-before-deciding-to-go-out-for-dinner thing, Lori had grown tired of the dating scene. As she watched her older daughter get ready for her first date she had the sobering thought that dating was truly for the young, who had all the time in the world and had not seen much. Because she was 36 years old, Lori yearned for a better way to meet men who met her criteria:

❦ *30–40 years old.* Young guys were great in bed, but Lori really did not have much of an interest in the latest hip-hop beef.

❦ *Children.* Brothers with children understood her dedication and responsibilities, and they did not require her full attention 24/7.

❦ *Divorced.* No confirmed bachelors need apply. Lori wanted someone who, like herself, had been married and was looking to get it right the second time around.

❦ *Career-driven.* No lackluster brothers without goals. Lori had worked hard on her career and wanted to have a brother in her life who was just as driven.

❦ *Fun.* No more stick-in-the-muds. Lori had left an okay marriage that just lacked spontaneity and fun. This time she would not settle for a mediocre or just-getting-by relationship.

A friend turned Lori on to using professional dating services. Initially Lori balked at the idea of having some outside consultant search down her dream brother, but when she went for the initial consultation she learned that the agency did it all: polled her on what she wanted in a man, screened potential dates for compatibility, and arranged quick lunch dates for her. The additional plus was that brothers paid for the service as well, and there's nothing like putting dollars into something in order to make sure that you are serious about seeing results.

Lori went on a few of these lunch dates and met some great brothers, but none who had the spark that she was looking for. But even Lori had to admit that these brothers were a much better match than any of the on-the-street hookups that she was famous for entertaining.

After some time Lori learned quickly how to tell if a brother was even worthy of the lunch date. About a month into using the service, Lori met Abraham, a 41-year-old business analyst with two college-age daughters. He was new to the area and, much like Lori, was interested in meeting someone great, not just a seat filler. After a few get-to-know-you dates Abraham and Lori slowly moved into the relationship phase. Ten months later the two are still dating, and Lori is happy that she was able to open herself up to a new way to meet a great brother.

Lori upgraded and diversified her dating tools. By doing this not only was she able to meet men more tailored to her tastes and interests, but she was also able to stop wasting time on bad methods that work only for those sampling the field, not those looking for quality love.

❧ TRUTHFUL LESSON

Dating comes in many different varieties. Don't stick to the same flavor.

❧ BARE NECESSITY

BE AN INNOVATOR; MIX UP YOUR DATING OPTIONS FOR GUARANTEED FUN AND FULFILLMENT.

TRUTH XII
PLAYING KEEP-AWAY

Love is all about being present and interested.

I am so happy that I finally get it.

—Morgan, 22

LaDawn:

My head is spinning right now. I have been involved for the last six months with a wonderful man who loves and appreciates me. We actually went to high school together, and now that we are both home from college we decided to reconnect. This man is a dream as far as the attention that he pays me and the way that we like many of the same things. There is only one area in our relationship that is lacking and that is the sex. I am far more experienced than he is, and sometimes he doesn't always hit the spot.

I am writing you today not to ask for sexual advice, but to ask what you do when you have every confidence in your man but there is a rumor on the street that makes you question your positive outlook. Recently I had a really good friend of mine come to me and ask me just how well I knew my man. It turns out that this particular friend is married to one of my man's college classmates, and this classmate swears that my man was gay during his college years. Although I am embarrassed that someone within my circle knows, I am not shocked by this revelation. My man has told me that in the past he had experimented with men, but he has assured me that it was a phase and not who he is today. However, I still see signs that he may want to be with a man—he has maintained close relationships with men from his college days, there are times that I cannot account for where he may be or whom he is with, and our sex life is not improving. The whole down-low thing has my head spinning, and I don't know what to do. I am with this man because he is good to me, comes from a great family, and will one day will be a great father. Should I stay with a great man in a world where great men are rare?

Sister, you are chasing the dream of an ideal man. This brother is probably as wonderful as you have stated, but you have to get real and realize that you cannot just turn off sexual desires. If the brother likes to sleep with men, that has not changed—he has simply placed that desire on the shelf until he can sneak around and do it, or until the temptation grows to such high levels that it explodes and he has to act on it. In either situation you will be hurt by something that you knowingly signed on for. This makes you look like a fool. You do not want to be a woman with a mortgage, kids, and years invested in a relationship when your husband comes out of the closet. So many people will get hurt just because you had to play it safe with a great guy who should have been a friend and never your lover.

Stop chasing this man and go out and find another man who is just as great—and who can be the full package. You don't have to settle for a great gay friend in order to have a great love. This brother loves you, but he will never love you the way that you want.

————

thirteen

≈✥≈

STOP CHASING UNAVAILABLE MEN

*T*ruth XII is especially for my 20-something sisters because they tend to get caught up in the cycle of the unavailable man a lot faster than more mature sisters. Unavailable men come in many forms:

- ❧ Married brothers
- ❧ Incarcerated brothers
- ❧ Living-with-someone brothers
- ❧ Career-obsessed brothers
- ❧ Gay brothers
- ❧ Addicted brothers

Each of these brothers has something else going on in his life that will always keep him from being totally yours. Now, the reason I say this particular truth is for young ladies is that it is so much easier for a young woman to enter into a relationship with a brother with one of the above conditions because she has the time and patience to wait it out and the mind-set that everything in life can be changed. More mature sisters have already been down this road a few times, and if they are sensible they take the first exit off this highway before permanently attaching themselves to this route.

I have been with many unavailable brothers, and I know firsthand how exciting, passionate, and fulfilling these relationships can be. It is the constant chase for more of his attention and love and the constant emotional reinforcement that you are all that he wants. My unavailable man of choice was the involved brother. For a few months I was truly addicted to the high of taking another woman's man. I know a lot of you will want to close the book now, but the truth is we all have some aspects of our past that we are not particularly proud of. I count myself not as a bad woman for being a man-stealer but as a better woman for knowing why I did it and how to break the pattern.

For me, chasing Brother Y was the ultimate high. He was married and had children, yet he was totally interested in getting with me. His pursuit was incredible: flowers, gifts, dinners, and tickets to any show in town. The sex was incredible because I was the vacation sex that he craved after a long season of the same old, same old served up over many years. I was Brother Y's fantasy—the woman he never could have had in college or high school, but with years of sexual/romantic experience, a great career, and a cultured mind, he was finally getting what he had wanted for so long and had thought was out of reach. In my mind I was having fun being the fantasy and being pursued. The game of the other woman is that you are constantly being told or shown that you are better than another lady, and what woman doesn't want to feel exceptional?

For three months it was the most fun I'd had in quite some time, but then the weirdness crept in. I started to see him out at times with his wife while shopping or going out to eat. She would call when we were together, or I would notice the car seat in the back of the car when we would go out. Slowly I was growing envious of a woman who had full access to him all the time (he moved away from me when she called), and I realized that maybe he was never going to choose me over her. In the beginning of the relationship I rejoiced in my freedom to do whatever I wanted without a traditional boyfriend in tow, but that quickly changed when I realized I was not getting Brother Y's best, just another woman's leftovers. Our relationship finally ended when one night we were talking in his car and I noticed a small jewelry bag stowed in the dash. I asked him if he had gotten his wife a gift, and he told me no—then he proceeded to open the box and show me that he had gotten her rings cleaned while she was out of town. Staring down at the most regal of wedding sets, I realized that he belonged to her. I was only a temporary fill-in until their relationship got strong again. I was close to getting out of the car at that point and ending things when Brother Y removed the rings from their case and told me that I could try them on if I wanted. At this point I knew that not only would this brother never be mine, but he had little if any respect for me and what I may have felt when being confronted with a symbol of his commitment to his wife. It was not Brother Y's fault that my feelings were hurt; he had held up his end of the deal, providing me with a satisfying fling. I was the one in the wrong here because I wanted and needed a love in total, yet I chose to link with half of a man.

On my radio show and Web site I get call after call and e-mail after e-mail from sisters trying to make that critical decision on whether to stay or go. When you dig into the story of the relationship, you quickly find out that sisters looking for love, monogamy, intimacy, and companionship have unwittingly linked themselves up to brothers who are just not able to be present in a relationship. Get Truth XII and you will save yourself a lot of disappointment and emotional stress down the road. Break the old habit of linking yourself to men who can never truly return the favor.

❧ TRUTH XII

STOP CHASING THE UNAVAILABLE BROTHER

Place your energy and attention on brothers who are accessible and interested.

THE LOWDOWN

So many sisters fall for unavailable brothers blindly or on purpose because the ultimate high is to make a man change and choose us. Unavailable men come in many forms, and we sisters have to be quick to identify them and move on to the next. While I would love to dig deeply into the many types of unavailable men, I think I will stick to three main ones that sisters seem to reach out to me about every day: married or involved men, gay men, and incarcerated men.

Married or Otherwise Involved Men

Every night I receive e-mails and phone calls from sisters wondering if they should stay in relationships with unavailable men. The main reason for their bewilderment is that the man often has a wife or a girlfriend and the sister is starting to realize that she may never be number one. In the case of being involved with a man who has another lady, sisters are constantly looking for actions, words, and commitments to prove that they are more important than the other woman. Sisters chase the involved man because winning him over means that they are the better sister.

When sisters reach out to me with this question about a married or otherwise involved man, my answer to them is always the same: "Why are you shortchanging yourself?" Every woman deserves to have a love in full. If a man has another more serious relationship in his life, she is getting his best and you are only getting what is left. If you really want this man to be yours, then let him go and ask him to decide where he really wants to be. It is only through forcing him to make the decision that you can have a clear answer on what he really thinks of you and the value that you bring to his life. From my very own personal experience I can tell you that there is a very short shelf life for sharing a man. You will always want more, and when you do, that is when feelings become hurt. Don't wait for the other shoe to fall. Know that you deserve more than chasing after someone else's man.

Gay or Bisexual Men

Recently there has been a lot of conversation about women who are unknowingly involved with men who are either gay or bisexual. But in my experience there is another group of sisters who get little if any attention: those who chase gay men hoping to make them straight. There is a growing group of sisters out there who have gay friends whom they truly love, and while they are out hanging with them every Saturday night they're secretly hoping that these men will realize that they aren't gay and that the ideal sister is sitting on the bar stool next to them. My mailbag overflows with letters from sisters who have slept with their best gay buddy and the sex wasn't awful and they woke and still liked each other next morning and should she marry him?

So many sisters have been so scared into believing the no-good-black-men myth that they are willing to accept a great friendship over passionate love just to have a brother and children in their lives. Ladies, please read this closely: *Not every great friend makes a great mate.* How many of us have turned away brothers that we liked hanging out with at the mall, at the movies, or at work because we knew that although they were great in many areas, they lacked that little something that would make them an excellent love match? Gay men fall within the same category. No matter how great the sex was that one time or how much you guys have in common, the fact remains that at the end of the day he desires to be linked intimately with a man. I do believe a gay man can maybe ignore these feelings for a time, the same way straight people can step away from sexual urges for a time, but I think it is inevitable that he will once again be with a man.

Now, if you are a sister who is comfortable and open enough sexually to know that your man will on occasion be with other men, then get your roll on. But most sisters who fall for gay guys really believe that they can love the gayness out of him and through providing a home and family, so that he will never look at another man again. Sister, please don't fool yourself—stop chasing gay men! They cannot turn off their homosexual urges any more than you can turn off your heterosexual ones. If you sign on to this deal, you are heading down a road of love that is filled with covert plans, hurt feelings, and sad results.

Incarcerated Men

The final unavailable man that I want to touch on is the brother who is locked up. Sisters, you are really holding it down for the brothers, and for every brother who gets out and changes his ways and steps up to the relationship plate, I applaud you for your high level of support and dedication. But there are some sisters out there who are crazy in love with brothers in prison but who are not going to get the great brother on the other side. These sisters give up their time, love, and dollars with no payoff because these brothers are not looking to be great lovers when they get out—they are looking only for support systems and entertainment while they are in.

Sisters, if any of the following things are occurring while your man is locked up, this may not be the best relationship for you:

❧ The brother is constantly hitting you up for money.
❧ There are other baby mamas or women coming to see him on the regular.
❧ He is disrespectful or mean to you while he is behind bars.
❧ He has no clear plan for what is going to happen to him or you when he gets out.

These are the clear signs that this brother does not plan on being yours when he gets out. Yet sisters hang in there hoping and praying for change, thinking that all of the pictures, sexy letters, and hot little outfits on visitation day will make their men more interested in them and better men when he comes out. Sister, it is not going to work out quite that way. If you doubt his love while he is behind bars, more than likely you will doubt it once again when he is released. Do not place your life in a holding pattern for this brother—he needs to focus on getting himself straight, while you deserve to live. So many sisters think holding it down for a brother on lockdown is a badge of honor when really it is a sign that you are not brave enough or self-assured enough to know that you deserve so much more.

MORGAN

Morgan is a frequent caller to my radio show who sends love out to her man, Steelo, who is on lockdown. Every night Morgan calls in and makes sure that her man knows that she loves him and will be up to see him over the weekend. My jail lovebirds rarely call in to the show for advice, so I basically assume that their nightly love dedications are a sign that they are happy in their relationships and that they want to just tell their man good night.

One night Morgan actually called in with a relationship question. She wanted to know if a woman should continue to support and visit a brother who was mean to her before he was locked up and has other women while he is in jail. Morgan wanted to know if Steelo was going to change back to the bad brother he was when he was out. At the heart of Morgan's question was an issue that many sisters deal with: "Is a brother using me?" When Morgan told me more about her relationship it became clear that this was a brother who had disrespected her when he was out, seeing other women, abusing her physically, and having an acute bad reaction to commitment. Since being locked up Steelo had been very loving and attentive, but he was still evasive when it came to how he really felt about Morgan and what their relationship would be like when he is released.

Recently Morgan noticed that Steelo still has a violent

and abusive nature, even behind bars. When she doesn't write back or call or doesn't have the funds to visit him, he is mean and aggressive with her. Morgan recently found out that she is the only person coming to see Steelo during his recent jail term because his family and friends have grown tired of him constantly getting locked up. Morgan was beginning to feel that Steelo needs her now only because he is locked up with no options. She felt that if he was free he would not have any interest in being with her.

I suggested to Morgan that she might want to sever this relationship because this brother seems to need a jailhouse romance and not a real-world one. He needs someone to rely on while he is in, but he appears to have few plans for when he gets out. Also, the fact that he is still showing his abusive nature on the inside means that there would absolutely be more abuse when he gets out. My whole conversation with Morgan boiled down to the fact that this brother was unavailable to her because he is still wrapped up in a mind-set that was going to keep him in and out of jail for the rest of his life. Steelo had not demonstrated any changes in his motivation or actions to show that he wanted a different type of life with Morgan on the outside. She needed to stop wasting her time with this brother and find someone within reach who could treat her much better.

Morgan realized that she was wasting valuable time on loving men who were never going to be hers. While every relationship does have its benefits, Morgan was unable to realize what she really wanted: an old-fashioned loving relationship. One day she woke up and realized that she was shortchanging herself by knowingly pursuing men who were unavailable to her.

❧ TRUTHFUL LESSON

Free yourself of the burden of maintaining limited relationships.

I want to speak honestly to sisters who are dealing with unavailable men no matter what the circumstances. Why are you wasting your time on a brother who can't be your partner in full? The real truth behind the unavailable man is that you are draining your body and mind with a relationship that will never totally fill you up. These unavailable relationships we often volunteer for, thinking that we can just handle it and eventually change it, rarely work out as planned. Little do we realize that we are just signing on for a relationship that has no way of ever being fulfilling. You deserve so much more, and you have to believe it.

❧ BARE NECESSITY

YOU DESERVE 100 PERCENT. DON'T ACCEPT ANYTHING LESS.

NOW YOU GET IT

Not only have I been able to have better relationships with men, but also my work and family relationships have improved. The truths have truly been eye-opening for me.

—Selena, 28

LaDawn,
Keep up the great work. I have written you several times about my drama-filled love life, and your answers have always been dead-on.

Thanks for the love. I really believe that each of us has the power to improve every aspect of our lives. We only have to take the proactive stance and move forward toward our desired end result.

fourteen

GET YOUR SHINE ON

*W*ow! Are we finished already? Since I have stripped you of your old ideas, now is the time to get dressed again in the finest of possibilities. You have read the truths and thought about how they apply to the way that you identify, pursue, and nurture a great relationship with the very best black man. In many ways you are probably thinking that these truths make such common sense, how could you have not known them before?

As I told you in the opening chapter, the truths are not groundbreaking. They are simply ideas that can greatly improve the quality of your life, thereby leading you to be interested in and attract only brothers who have the same high standard of living—a simple concept that can reap huge rewards. My goal in presenting the truths to you is for you to think a little more about the ways that you can improve yourself so that you can live your ideal life. If you are happy and fulfilled, others will automatically be drawn to you, hoping to catch some of the glow. Sisters, it is time to shine!

I challenge you now to really put into action the ideas behind the truths. Proactively change the quality of life that you lead. Step away from the waiting area and step onto the platform of motion. Move toward the relationship and love that you deserve, knowing that not only are you deserving of the best, but you can also be the best for the very best black man.

The truths are only the starting point. Now the hard work begins—the work of changing the way that you view your role and responsibilities in relationships and identifying those things around you that may be working contrary to your plan. It's time to clean your relationship house and strip away bad perceptions and practices. The time is now to start getting the high quality of love that you deserve. The truths will get you where you need to go.

Get to work!

CHEAT SHEET
FOR THE TRUTHS

I. Let Go of the Past
I will take today on its own merits.

II. Gain a Sense of Fun
Today I will try something new.

III. Make Your Relationship a Priority
I will give myself space.

IV. Sex Is Not a Four-Letter Word
I am responsible for my ultimate pleasure.

V. Get the Clues
I will listen in total to the world around me.

VI. Be the Prize
I am a unique creation worthy of praise.

VII. Break the Girlfriend Chain
I will remove from my life people who drain me.

VIII. Live for You
The power to be happy comes from me.

IX. Friendship Truly Matters
I will only be involved with those whom I genuinely like.

X. Always Remember the First Time

I will use my beginnings as fuel for my future.

XI. Get into the Dating Mix

Be an innovator; mix up your dating options for guaranteed fun and fulfillment.

XII. Playing Keep-away

You deserve 100 percent—don't accept anything less.

GET EVEN MORE STRIPPED

Stripped Bare Books

Visit www.ladawnblack.com for:

- Love Q & A—Just for You
- Great Love-Themed Gifts
- Dates for the Good Luv'N Tour, relationship seminars, and book tour
- To submit a relationship question to LaDawn Black
- To book LaDawn Black for your next event
- To rate *Stripped Bare* and leave personal stories and letters that may be used in future publications
- And last but not least to celebrate black love in all of its forms 24/7

I wish you the best in life and love and I look forward to hearing from you soon!

—*LaDawn*

ABOUT THE AUTHOR

*R*elationship advice now has a fresh new voice. LaDawn Black, relationship expert, author, and radio and television personality has dedicated herself to the mission of showing women the ways that they can control the quality of the love in their lives.

A native of Washington, D.C., LaDawn Black was recently voted Best Radio Personality in Baltimore and is the host of Baltimore's number-one-rated relationship and sex advice show—*The Love Zone* on WERQ (92.3 FM). In addition to her *Love Zone* show, Black is also the featured relationship expert for the *Carter and Sanborn* morning radio show in Philadelphia. Black is also the chief relationship advice strategist for Blackmeninamerica.com and contributes advice columns and tips to several urban lifestyle publications, online magazines, and relationship websites. Black currently resides in Baltimore, Maryland, with her two very best black men, her husband, JB, and son, Alec.